Wellington's Early Peninsula Campaigns

WELLINGTON

Wellington's Early Peninsula Campaigns
A Serving Officer's History
1808-1811

John Fane

Wellington's Early Peninsula Campaigns:
A Serving Officer's History 1808-1811
by John Fane

Originally published in 1820 under the title
*Memoir of the Early Campaigns of the Duke of Wellington
in Portugal and Spain*

Leonaur is an imprint of Oakpast Ltd

Material original to this edition and
presentation of text in this form
copyright © 2010 Oakpast Ltd

ISBN: 978-0-85706-359-5 (hardcover)
ISBN: 978-0-85706-360-1 (softcover)

http://www.leonaur.com

Publisher's Notes

The views expressed in this book are not necessarily
those of the publisher.

Contents

Introduction	7
Rolica	9
Vimiera	18
Armistice	26
Corunna	34
Oporto	42
Talavera	47
Almonacid	60
Ocaña	68
Andalusia	76
The Coa & Almeida	83
Busaco	97
The Lines at Torres Vedras	105
Massena in Retreat	119
Albuhera & Fuentes d'Honor	129

Introduction

The following sheets pretend to no merit in composition, the writer pretends to no reputation as an author; the subject must be interesting to every British reader, and if the events are faithfully recorded, the work will deserve some attention.

Unaccustomed for a series of years to any great or continued exertion upon the continent, the people of England almost doubted their power or means of supporting one. The genius of Lord Wellington, the bravery of British troops, have removed this doubt.

To the detail of the brilliant exploits by which the early campaigns in Portugal and Spain were distinguished, this work is dedicated. The author has undertaken it, emboldened by the consideration, that from the opportunities which he enjoyed of observing the transactions in the Peninsula, in most of which he was personally engaged, he has the means of relating them correctly.

Chapter 1

Rolica

In the summer of 1808 the first deputies from, the Asturias arrived in England; they were so rapidly succeeded by others from every part of the Peninsula, that after a very short time there remained, no doubt that the great people, whom they came to represent, were determined to struggle for independence. The British ministers did no more than echo the sentiments of the nation when they decided to give every support to this people and Sir Arthur Wellesley, who had been appointed to the command of a corps destined for a different service, was selected to lead the first armament which should carry assistance to Portugal and Spain.

The force under his orders sailed from Cork in the beginning of July; Sir Arthur Wellesley himself proceeded in a single ship to Corunna. The state of things upon his arrival at that port was unfavourable to the Spaniards. The Galician army under Blake, and that of Castile under Cuesta, had been defeated by a French corps commanded by Marshal Bessieres, in the neighbourhood of Rio-Seco; and there appeared no obstacle to the march of the enemy to Corunna. In this situation of affairs Sir Arthur Wellesley hinted to the Junta, that if a request to land his army for the protection of Galicia should be made to him, he would not hesitate in acceding to it. The Junta, however, actuated by a feeling of pride and jealousy which has so often brought the affairs of Spain to the brink of ruin, neglected to make this proposal. Sir Arthur consequently proceeded to the coast of Portugal, and arrived in Mondego Bay on the 26th of July. Leaving there the expedition he commanded, he went to the mouth of the Tagus, to procure information, and to combine his operations with Admiral Sir C. Cotton. When these objects were accomplished, he returned to the Mondego, determining to land his troops as soon as the corps which he expected, either from Cadiz, under General Spencer, or from England, under General Ackland, should have arrived. The former joined on the 2nd of August; and Sir Arthur Wellesley immediately disembarked his army. At this moment three-fourths of Portugal were in insurrection against the French. Junot, who had entered the country in the November preceding, had commanded a corps of 40,000 men, of which about 10,000 were Spaniards; Oporto was occupied by a part of the Spanish troops, the rest of them were at Lisbon.

At the commencement of the revolution in Spain, Junot entertained so great a suspicion of the Spaniards in that capital, and in its neighbourhood, that, under pretence of sending them to other quarters, he succeeded in surrounding and disarming them, and afterwards in placing them as prisoners on board ships provided for that purpose in the Tagus. As soon as the intelligence of this event reached Oporto, the Spanish garrison seized the few French officers who were in the town; invited the inhabitants to follow the example of Spain, and resist the French; and themselves marched off to join their companions in Galicia.

The Portuguese had, however, before this time, raised the standard of their prince. The Bishop of Oporto assumed the government of the northern provinces of Portugal; and General Frere and other persons took the lead in the insurrection in the other parts of that country. The old soldiers, who had been disbanded by the French, were called to arms; and in a short time three armies were formed; one at Oporto, another at Coimbra, and the third at Viseu. Officers had already been despatched from England to ascertain the state of the Oporto and Coimbra corps; and Sir Arthur Wellesley sent an officer to Viseu to report to him the state of the force assembled there under General Barcellar. It is needless to observe, that an army formed as the Portuguese had been, could not be very effective, such as it was, however, it was hearty in the cause of its country, and most anxious for an opportunity of revenging the wrongs which had been inflicted upon the nation.

The corps of Oporto was joined to that of Coimbra, and was destined to act with Sir Arthur Wellesley. The corps of Viseu was sent to Guarda; whence, in conjunction with some Spaniards under the orders of the Marquis of Valadares, it was directed to march upon Abrantes, and from thence cooperate in the meditated attack on Lisbon. There was also a corps of Spaniards of some force collected at Badajos under General Galluzzo, which it was hoped might have given some assistance to these combinations, by a simultaneous operation in the Alemtejo.

Such was the state of the allied force when Sir Arthur Wellesley first landed his army on the banks of the Mondego. The French were in possession of Lisbon, and the country north of it as far as Leyria, which had been recaptured from the Portuguese by a force under the orders of General Margaron. On the entry of the French into this town, they committed the most atrocious acts of cruelty.[1] As an instance of the brutality of a superior officer, the —— of —— related of himself, that upon entering the town, he met a woman with a child at her breast, that the appearance of the infant excited his pity, but *se rapellant qu'il etait soldat*, he pierced the two bodies with a single thrust of his sword. When the English advanced-guard arrived there, it found in one of the convents the dead bodies of several monks, who had been killed by the French soldiers; some of whom had

---

1. The cruelties committed by the French army in this instance, and throughout the whole of its campaigns in Portugal, had their origin in the nature of the war in which it was now for the first time engaged. Till this period, wherever the French soldiers had established themselves, whether by the defeat of the armies which defended the country invaded, or otherwise, they found the people submitting to their rule; when, in Portugal, therefore, the nation rose in hostility against them, they considered such resistance as rebellion, and looked upon the inhabitants taken in arms, as disturbers of the public peace, and therefore entitled to no mercy or consideration. The officers also hoped, by inflicting vengeance on the patriots, to arrest the progress of an insurrection which menaced their total overthrow. It would not be fair to argue, from the conduct of the French in Portugal, that in other situations they would be led to adopt similar proceedings.

dipped their hands in the blood of their unfortunate victims, and had daubed with it the walls of the convent.

To the southward of the Tagus, the French had been unable to retain any part of the Alemtejo.

About the end of July, Junot detached a corps, under the orders of General Loison, to repress, in the first instance, the insurrections of that province; next, to give whatever assistance might be wanted by the garrison of Elvas; and, lastly, to return by Abrantes to the north of the Tagus, and to wreak a signal vengeance upon Coimbra. General Loison, in execution of these directions, marched to Evora, where the Portuguese had collected the. force of the provinces, and, assisted by: some Spaniards, resolved to defend the town. General Loison attacked it, and after meeting with a considerable resistance, entered it, and delivered it over to pillage. The inhabitants, threatened with indiscriminate massacre, endeavoured to shelter themselves in the churches and convents, where they had been accustomed to look for protection; but this was of no avail against their merciless enemies; thousands of them were drawn from their places of refuge, and fell victims to a licentious soldiery, excited by the unrestrained desire of plunder and revenge.

From Evora, General Loison marched to Elvas, and from thence returned by Abrantes to Thomar, where he was arrested in the further execution of his instructions, by the news that Sir Arthur Wellesley had landed and was at Leyria, upon his march towards Lisbon.

During this period Sir Arthur had prepared for the campaign he was about to undertake.

He had 13,000 British infantry and 300 cavalry; he selected 5,000 of the best Portuguese troops that were assembled at Coimbra, and with an army so composed, determined to move forward. He was in daily expectation of a corps of 5,000 men from England, and he was also apprized that the body of men who had been under Lieut.-General Moore in Sweden, had received orders to proceed to the Peninsula.

The Commissariat, under Sir Arthur Wellesley, was defective;

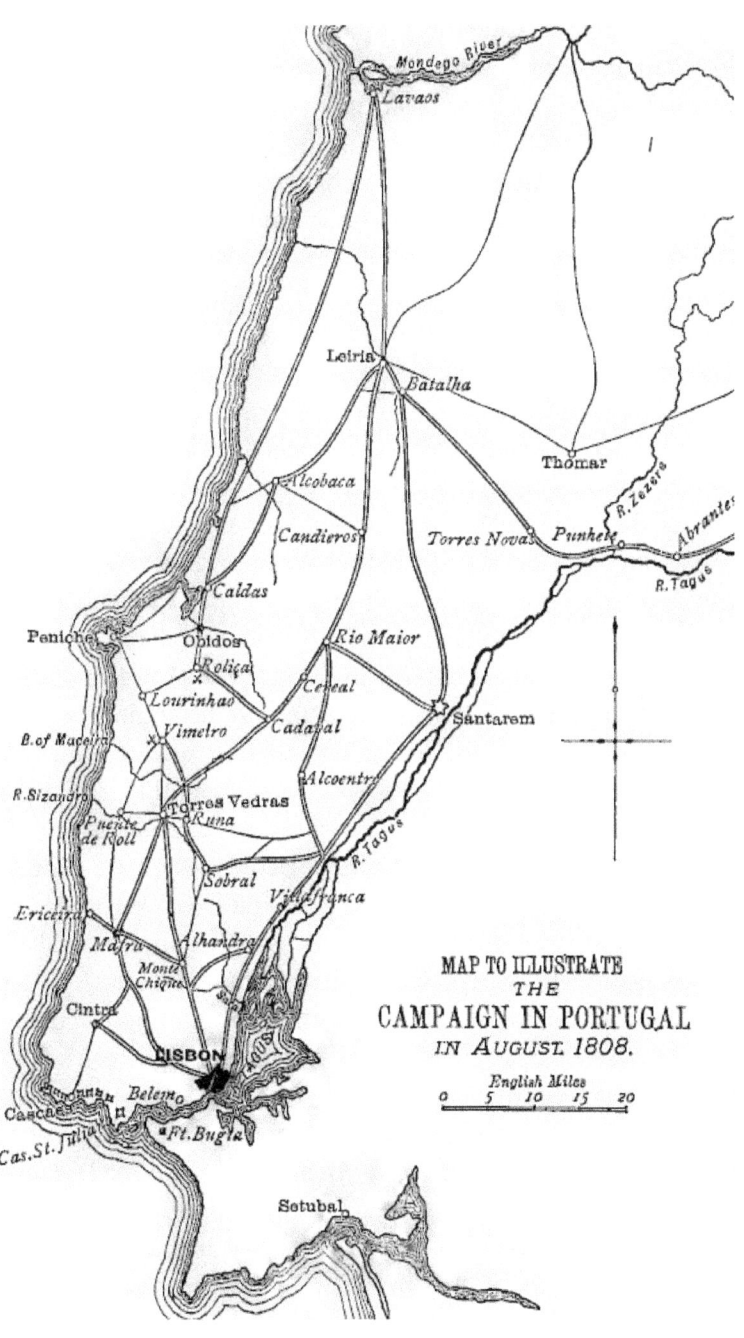

an army just landed must necessarily be without the means of transport; it was, therefore, evident that it must depend entirely upon its communication with the shipping for its support throughout its operations: Sir Arthur Wellesley upon these considerations determined to advance by the road nearest the coast; by that movement he secured to himself the advantages of being able to receive his reinforcements at any time they should arrive; and in addition, he was not cramped by any line of communication which it would be necessary for him to maintain, or which he must have defended, had the enemy (as was once contemplated) made any demonstrations upon his rear.

Before he quitted the Mondego, he left instructions for the corps under General Ackland to proceed along the coast to join him. He also left a statement, of the information he had obtained, and of the opinions he had formed, to be delivered to Sir John Moore upon his arrival. Sir Arthur Wellesley recommended, that the corps under that officer should be landed in the Mondego, and marched to Santarem, so as to operate to the southward of the Tagus, if necessary, and to prevent the enemy from retiring through the province of Alemtejo, in case he should be beaten by the force which Sir Arthur was leading against him. Other objects were in contemplation, but these were the principal.

This proposed system of operations was afterwards subjected to considerable discussion; it was objected to, and set aside. The mind, however, which conceived it, would have executed it with success, though in other hands it might appear impracticable. The battle of Vimiera, in which only half the force under Sir Arthur Wellesley was engaged, proved the correctness of his calculations, and warrants a belief that if the whole campaign had been directed according to his views, the result would have proved more advantageous than it did under a different arrangement.

On the 9th of August, Sir Arthur Wellesley made his first movement from the Mondego, and reached Leyria on the 10th; he halted two days to make the necessary arrangements for his advance, and to bring up the Portuguese who were at Coimbra. On the 13th he moved to the ground about Batalha, where a patrol of French, from the corps under General La Borde, at Alcobaca, was first discovered. General Frere, who commanded the Portuguese, here made an objection to advance any further, stating, as his reason, the improbability of finding provisions. Sir Arthur Wellesley was not disconcerted by this defection: after attempting in vain to alter General Frere's determination, he decided to move forward, taking with his army a detachment of 1,600 men, from the force under that officer's command, which he placed under the orders of Colonel Trant, and which Sir Arthur undertook to provision. These arrangements being made, he advanced to attack the corps that occupied Alcobaca; the enemy had, however, abandoned it in the night, and the British army took up its position upon the heights beyond it. The next day the army moved forward to Caldas; the advance, under Brigadier General Fane, to Obidos; where some skirmishing took place between the light troops under his orders, and the French rear.

On the 17th Sir Arthur Wellesley moved to attack General La Borde, who had not as yet been joined by the force under General Loison, which was marching by Alemquer, to effect that object. General La Borde was posted at Rolica, in a strong position upon some heights which covered the road from Obidos to Lisbon.

Sir Arthur first formed his army in columns of battalions, behind Obidos, from thence he detached the light troops, under Brigadier-General H. Fane, supported by Major General Ferguson's brigade, along some heights which led to the right of the enemy's position. The rest of the army passed through Obidos, and advanced along the plain towards Rolica.

The enemy was first discovered, drawn up at the foot of the hill, and in front of the position; but upon seeing our advance he retired to the heights.

Sir Arthur, upon a close examination of the ground thus taken up, and wishing to prevent the possibility of General La Borders retiring upon the fortress of Peniche, determined to advance the right of his army as well as the left, and thus to attack both flanks of the enemy's position. The attack on the enemy's left was led on by the brigade under Major General Hill, while the 45th and 29th Regiments under Major General Nightingale were ordered to advance upon the centre; Major General Ferguson's brigade was brought from the heights on the left into the plain, to support this movement; by continuing however its original direction, that corps might have rendered more essential service, since it would have fallen upon the French right, and in conjunction with Brigadier General Fane's corps, would have decided the fate of, the action sooner: but some mistake having arisen in an order delivered to it, this advantage was not obtained.

The 29th Regiment ascended the hill by a hollow way which led to the summit, and encountered, a most determined resistance on the height where the enemy was formed. The path along which the regiment moved was so narrow, as to admit but three or four men abreast; so that when it had reached the ground upon which it was to deploy, the soldiers were exposed to the fire of the French corps which occupied the vineyards, while they were unable to form any front, from which to return it; the grenadier company, however, charged that part of the enemy which was upon the open, and by that act of heroism, (although it was afterwards driven back by the fire from the vineyards), gave time to some of the companies behind it to form, and to maintain the ground they had got possession of. In the meantime, the light troops, under Brigadier General Fane, had got upon the right of the position, and Major General Hill had ascended the hill upon its left; so that the enemy was obliged to abandon his first line, and retire into the village of Zambugera in the rear.

From this he was driven by a most gallant charge under the direction of Major General Spencer, which terminated the action.

General La Borde continued to make some resistance upon a height beyond the village, only for the purpose of collecting and forming his troops in the plain behind it, which he executed with considerable ability. After having formed them upon two lines he retired, filing from his left upon the road to Torres Vedras.

Such was the first battle fought by British troops in the great cause of the Peninsula: it cost us some valuable lives, among whom Colonel Lake and Captain Bradford were the most distinguished; but it gave a sample of that bravery and good conduct which have since marked the progress of our arms, and have raised the military renown of England to the glorious eminence on which it at present stands. The advantage which resulted from this action was great. General Loison was marching to join General La Borde, in the position of Rolica; his columns, the next day, were distinctly perceived in the direction of Torres Vedras, to which place he was forced to retire, in consequence of the action of the preceding morning; but if the two corps had been at the battle of Rolica, the British loss must have been considerably greater, and the general operations of the campaign proportionally delayed.

Chapter 2
Vimiera

The following day, the 18th, Sir Arthur Wellesley marched the army to Lourinhal, for the purpose of bringing supplies from the shipping, as also to receive the reinforcements which were understood to be upon the coast from England.

The 19th he moved to Vimiera, on which day, the brigade under the orders of General Anstruther landed, and on the morning of the 20th marched up to the army. Sir Arthur Wellesley had during the last two clays supplied his army with provisions, had received part of his reinforcements, and directed the rest which were in the offing, under Major General Ackland, to land in the course of the night; he determined, therefore, to move forward to Mafra, and the orders to that effect were given.

The enemy was known to have collected his force at Torres Vedras; his cavalry had patrolled about the British army during the preceding days, without being opposed; the superiority of numbers in that arm was decided.

But Sir Arthur Wellesley conceived that by moving along the coast road to Mafra, he should turn the position which the French occupied, and by that operation force them to retire upon Lisbon. He was also of opinion, that from the rapidity of his own march, he should arrive in the neighbourhood of that town, before the enemy would be able to occupy, with advantage, the ground which would defend it, and upon which he should force them to give him battle. On the evening of this day, however, a frigate, on board which was Sir Harry Burrard, arrived in Marciera Bay; Sir Arthur Wellesley immediately waited on that officer, to receive his orders, and to communicate to him the plans he was about to pursue, Sir Harry Burrard disapproved of them, directed counter orders to be issued to the army, to prevent its march in the morning, and determined to await the arrival of the corps under the orders of Sir John Moore. Sir Arthur Wellesley represented that the French army was now so near, that it was impossible to prevent an action; that the corps under his orders was equal to the contest with it; that the army of Sir John Moore would be of infinitely more service by marching upon Santarem; and that the greatest disadvantage would arise, from our changing at once from an offensive to a defensive line of operations. Sir Harry Burrard remained, however, fixed to his first intention; the counter orders were given, and a messenger was despatched to Sir John Moore, to direct him to move down in his transports, to Marciera Bay. Thus was the whole system of our campaign changed in a moment. With the enemy collected within three leagues of us, we were directed to remain stationary, till a corps of which we had, as yet, no tidings, should arrive.

The event; however, proved what Sir Arthur Wellesley had foretold. At nine in the morning of the 21st, our advanced posts were attacked, and the glorious battle of Vimiera evinced that the British army was worthy of the confidence which its General had reposed in it, in the discussion of the preceding evening.

Early on this day, Sir Arthur Wellesley had been to the advanced posts, and had returned to his quarters, when the first shots were exchanged with the advance of the enemy, who had passed from Torres Vedras, through the defile in front of it, and had been marching during the whole of the night.

Sir Arthur Wellesley had posted the light troops and the 50th Regiment, under Brigadier General Fane, upon a height near a windmill, in front of the village of Vimiera. Brigadier. General Anstruther was upon the right of this corps, but a part of his brigade was detached during the action, to occupy Vimiera; the left of the army was placed upon a ridge of heights, which run eastward into the country, and across which the brigades of Major General Ferguson and Major General Nightingale were

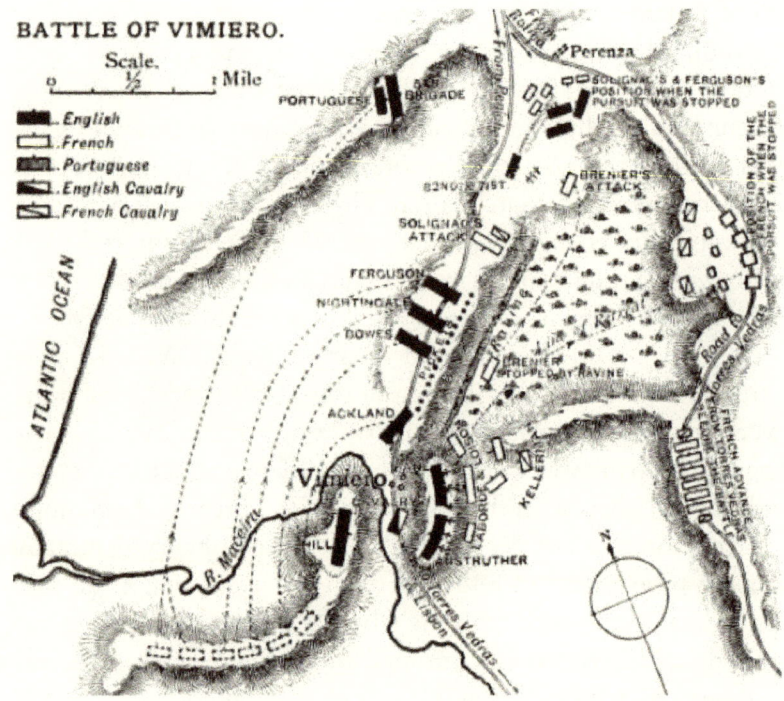

placed in position. The rest of the army was in reserve, upon heights in rear of Vimiera, which in reality formed the position, the one in which the action was fought being only the advance of it. The French army was divided into two divisions, under Generals La Borde and Loison, and the reserve, composed of the grenadiers and light infantry, together with the cavalry, under General Kellerman.

Junot separated his army, to attack the positions of our right and left at the same moment, connecting his two wings by the force under General Kellerman; they were, however, at too great a distance from each other, and their attacks were unconnected.

The left column was first engaged with the brigade of Brigadier General Anstruther; it attempted to turn his right, but after a contest of some duration, in which the superiority of the British fire, in the first instance, and afterwards of British bayonets, was completely proved, the enemy was repulsed with great slaughter, and forced to abandon his undertaking. The right column (which had moved to the left of the British) began its attack upon the brigades of Major Generals Ferguson and Nightingale, at the time that the left had been beaten by Brigadier General Anstruther. It commenced with considerable vigour, but the steadiness with which it was received, soon stopped its career; in less than half an hour the column was beaten, and pursued beyond the heights; General Bregnier and six guns taken. A French regiment afterwards rallied near the village of Ventoso, at the extremity of the hill, and made an attack, in column of mass, to recover the guns; but it was completely routed, with great loss. The attack upon the village of Vimiera, as the decisive effort, was made by the reserve, in close column, supported by artillery, but was most gallantly resisted by the 50th and part of the 43rd Regiments, who charged the flank of the column and totally defeated it. Two squadrons of the 20th Regiment of cavalry moved upon it when broken, and cut down and took prisoners a considerable number of those composing it, who were escaping from the infantry.

A short time before the victory was decided, Sir Harry Burrard arrived from the frigate, on board which he had remained during the night; Sir Arthur Wellesley was preparing to follow up the advantages he had gained; and had already brought up Brigadier General Bowes and Major General Ackland's brigades, (who had as yet been in the reserve and unengaged) with which he had intended to pursue the enemy. He had also directed Major General Hill to be ready to move from his right along a road which he was in possession of, and which led by the nearest line to Torres Vedras. But Sir Harry Burrard, conceiving that such a movement would be attended with risk, desired Sir Arthur Wellesley to discontinue the pursuit, and to rest satisfied with the advantages that had been gained.

Sir Arthur Wellesley remonstrated on the field against the order to halt, but it was of no avail; the decision was not to be changed or modified; the enemy retired at his leisure; our light troops even were not ordered to attend his movements, and a part of the rear-guard remained upon a hill within a short distance of our position till the following morning.

Without wishing to cast any reflection upon the conduct of Sir Harry Burrard, admitting that (called upon to take the command of an army already considerably advanced in the operations it had undertaken, and so nearly in contact with the collected force of the enemy as to make an action inevitable), he was placed in a situation of great difficulty; yet it is impossible not to regret that the person, in whose mind the plan of the campaign originally was formed, was not allowed to execute it throughout.

The system which Sir Arthur Wellesley had laid down had now been altered in three most essential points. First, the not proceeding on the morning of the 21st to turn the left of the enemy, by the movement he had ordered upon Mafra; thereby changing the operations of the army from the offensive to the defensive. Secondly, the not pursuing the enemy after the victory of Vimiera; and, lastly, the having changed the direction of Lieutenant General Sir John Moore's corps, from its march upon Santarem to its junction with the army of Sir Arthur Wellesley.

It may not be uninteresting to trace the probable effects which these movements would have produced.

General Junot had taken the command of the whole disposable force under his orders in Portugal (amounting to 14,000 men), at Torres Vedras on the 20th; and presuming upon the boasted superiority of French troops to those of any other nation, he had resolved to attack the left of the British army, thereby leaving it no retreat if defeated, but to the sea-shore, and to its transports, if it could effect its, embarkation. With this intention he marched on the night of the 20th by a road leading through a most difficult defile, which brought him to the eastward of Vimiera, near which place he arrived soon after nine-o'clock on the 21st. The order which had been issued the day before for the British army was to march at five-o'clock, by the road to the Ponte de Roll, and from thence direct upon Mafra. This road was separated about two leagues from that upon which the French army was advancing, and leading in a totally different direction; divided also from it by a woody and almost impervious tract of country; so that if the movement had been executed, the British army would have been considerably advanced towards Mafra, before the enemy had arrived at Vimeira.

If indeed this march had been discovered by the French patrols, it would still have been impossible to arrest our progress, from the difficulty of getting to us; and in all probability, the enemy would have had no other resource than to have returned to Torres Vedras (where the whole of his baggage had remained), and from thence tried to attack us at Mafra, which would have been attempted under many disadvantages; or to have marched in the greatest haste by the Cabeca de Montachique to have covered Lisbon. To those who are acquainted with the country I am speaking of, the difficulty of such movements (with an army which had already been marching since the morning of the 20th), will be duly appreciated: if the attempt to cover the capital had been made, the confusion and hurry with which a position must have been taken up would have bid fair for the success of our attack upon it, which could not have been delayed beyond the 23rd; the proximity of Lisbon, which was ripe for insurrection, must have added to the difficulties of the enemy; and upon a review of all the circumstances of the case, together with the great talents which Sir Arthur Wellesley has since displayed, we may be warranted in believing that complete success would have attended his operation; and that the possession of Lisbon would have been effected with a smaller loss, with greater advantages, and at a much earlier period, than it was obtained by the system which was adopted.

The next point to be considered is the effect which would have been produced by following up the enemy after the victory of Vimiera. General Junot had advanced from Torres Vedras by a circuitous road to Vimiera; and after his defeat the corps under Major General Hill, which had taken no part in the action, was in possession of the direct road to that place. The ground about Torres Vedras is extremely strong; and it is the only good pass by which the French army could have retired to Lisbon. Sir Arthur Wellesley was convinced that Major General Hill might have occupied the town before the enemy could have reached it; and that he might have defended the positions about it, till the army which was to have followed the French should have been able to communicate with him.

The great objection that was raised to this project was, that the British army was almost destitute of cavalry, whilst the French had of that arm a force of at least 1,200 men; but Sir Arthur Wellesley relied upon his own genius to provide a remedy to this objection; our infantry was in the best order, and it has too often since been tried in presence of a superior cavalry, to leave doubt in the mind of any British officer, that (if judiciously managed and supported with artillery), it is competent to advance in the face of cavalry. If, therefore, Sir Arthur Wellesley's intentions had been carried into effect, the probability is, that General Hill would have taken the enemy's baggage at Torres Vedras; that pursued by the British army, General Junot would have been unable to force the positions about that town; that he must, consequently, have retired by some other road, and his army have been subjected to considerable loss.

There remains only for us to consider the effects produced, by bringing the corps under the orders of Sir John Moore to Marceira Bay, instead of allowing it to proceed to Santarem.

Sir Arthur Wellesley had from the first conceived, that the corps under his immediate command was as considerable as could conveniently be employed upon the advance to Lisbon, and was of sufficient force to secure the success of that operation; but he foresaw that it would be impossible for him to prevent the French army from retiring through the Alemtejo, to Elvas, unless he could bring a separate corps to intercept it; with that view he had recommended the march of Sir John Moore upon Santarem, and that excellent officer, upon his arrival in Mondego Bay, disembarked a considerable portion of his troops with the view of executing that movement.

From the moment Sir Arthur Wellesley was apprized of the determination of Sir Harry Burrard to prevent that operation, and found himself arrested in his pursuit of the enemy after the battle of Vimiera, he gave up all hope of enclosing the French in Lisbon, or of preventing their protracting the campaign (if they thought fit to do so) by a movement into the southern provinces of Portugal.

Chapter 3

Armistice

We must now proceed to the relation of the events which took place after the battle of Vimiera.

Sir Arthur Wellesley employed himself, in the evening of the 21st, in getting stores and provisions landed for the troops, and strenuously urged an advance on the 22nd; but on the morning of that day, he was informed that Sir Hew Dalrymple was arrived in Marceira Bay, and was landing, to take the command. This officer soon afterwards reached Vimiera; he gave directions for the advance of the army on the next day; but about three-o'clock in the afternoon, General Kellerman arrived at the advanced posts, and requested a conference with the English commander-in-chief. Some officers were directed to conduct him to headquarters, with the persons who, formed his suite; and soon afterwards he proposed the terms to Sir Hew Dalrymple, upon which General Junot was prepared to conclude an armistice, with a view to his total evacuation of Portugal.

General Kellerman insisted much upon the still remaining strength; of the French army; that 10,000 Russians were prepared to land from the squadron which was in: the port of Lisbon, and to assist in the defence of Portugal; that General Junot (in possession of the fortresses, and with his movements upon Elvas undisturbed) was not in a situation to be dictated to, as to the terms upon which he was willing to evacuate the country; that although a part of the French army Had been repulsed from the position of the British, it still possessed considerable resources; that it had the opportunity of occupying, undisturbed, the positions which had been marked out for the defence of Lisbon; it therefore commanded respect; but that General Junot was willing to surrender the entire kingdom, with, the ports and fortresses, upon condition that the French army should be sent, with its whole military baggage, and at the expense of England, to its own country.

Sir Arthur Wellesley had conceived from the first, that the policy of Great Britain was to bring as early as possible to the assistance of the Spaniards, who were now upon the Ebro, the British army that was occupied in Portugal.

The plan upon which he had commenced that campaign was formed with that intention; the hope of seeing it accomplished, by force of arms, was now nearly, at an end. The march of the French Emperor into Spain was already talked of; and there seemed to be no hope, if the French were determined to protract the campaign in, Portugal, that a British army, after having beaten them in the field, and besieged the fortresses they occupied in the country, could, arrive in time to be of any assistance to the Spaniards. If, on the contrary, the terms proposed for the evacuation of Portugal were. agreed to, the embarkation of the enemy might be immediately effected, and the British, army might in a short, time be marched to the assistance of the Spaniards.

With this view of the various circumstances of the moment, Sir Arthur Wellesley gave his voice in favour of the principle of the armistice proposed; the minor details of it were objected to by him, particularly the wording of the article which related to the baggage, and which might be construed into a permission to carry off the plunder of Portugal; but it was thought, (after an understanding with General Kellerman, that it included only the baggage *"purement militaire"*) that the most proper moment for its correction, would be, in the arrangement of the convention.

With this explanation Sir Arthur Wellesley in pursuance of Sir Hew Dalrymple's directions; signed the Armistice.

It would be needless to relate here the terms of a document, which gave rise afterwards to so much discussion in England, and which must consequently be in the recollection of every Englishman. The period of the armistice was, two days, with twenty-four hours' notice of its rupture, and it precluded the British army from advancing beyond the line of the Zizandra. To give an opinion upon its merits would be presumption; but if the opportunity which it afforded of preparing the British army for its advance into Spain had been properly made use of, and if the execution of this object had not been so considerably delayed, by the tardiness of the embarkation of the French, it is probable that greater advantages would have resulted from it, than have generally been brought into consideration, in the discussions which it has occasioned.

The morning after the signature of the armistice, the British army advanced to Ramalhal. Colonel Murray was sent into the French headquarters, to discuss the terms of the convention, and the French retired from Torres Vedras to their positions in the vicinity of Lisbon. After the lapse of some days, the corps of Sir John Moore arrived in Marceira bay, and was landed near Vimiera. The following days it was advanced, and the whole army moved into Torres Vedras. The second day from its entrance into that place, Sir Arthur Wellesley, was directed to proceed with the corps with which he originally landed, to the town of Sobral, which commanded one of the great passes to Lisbon: on his march to that place he received a message from Sir Hew Dalrymple, informing him that Colonel Murray had arrived with the convention which he had signed, and that Sir Hew was prepared to ratify it.

The feeling of the army which had fought the battle of Vimiera, was at this time most hostile to the armistice which had been agreed upon.

The expression of a private in one of the regiments which had most gallantly asserted the superiority of the British arms, deserves to be recorded: whilst marching in his column to Sobral, he appeared to be looking for something which he had lost; and upon being asked what he was in search of, replied, *ten days,* which he believed he should never find again.

Sir Arthur Wellesley took up the ground about Sobral, with the corps which he commanded; a patrol of French fired upon one of his piquets, but upon its being returned, retired. The second day, Sir Arthur Wellesley moved on to Bucellas, where a line; of demarcation was drawn between the British and French posts.

The corps under the orders of Sir John Moore marched from Torres Vedras to Mafra. The leading division, under Major General the Honourable Edward Paget, had nearly reached that place, when a French officer, who commanded a piquet in the town, desired that the English army would not advance, as he had no orders to retire; the circumstance was reported to Sir Hew Dalrymple; who attempted to persuade the French officer to evacuate, but finding his efforts ineffectual, and being desirous to avoid engaging in any fresh hostilities, he ordered his troops to bivouac, for the night, on the ground they occupied. The next morning the French officer sent word that he had received orders to retire with his 100 men and that the British army was at liberty to enter the town. This story was the occasion of much witticism among the soldiers.

From Mafra, Sir Hew Dalrymple removed his headquarters to Cintra; from thence to the village of Acyras, near Fort St. Julian's; and from thence to Aquinto, between Paco d'Aquas and Lisbon, where he remained till the embarkation of the French army had been completed.

After the signature of the convention by Sir Hew Dalrymple, at Torres Vedras, and not at Cintra, as has generally been supposed two officers, Major General Beresford and Lord Proby; were sent into Lisbon to superintend its execution. The history of their disputes with the French would hardly be believed. It would be interesting to record them, as instances from which the characters of many of the individuals belonging to the French army might be collected, and the value of their point of honour appreciated.

The first object to which the attention of the British commissioners for the execution of the convention was drawn, was to enforce the spirit of that instrument, by preventing the French from carrying off the plunder of Portugal. With this view General Junot, after much opposition on his. Part, was constrained to issue an order to his army, requiring it to deliver up, into the hands of the commissioners appointed for that purpose, every species of plundered property which it retained in its possession. Within a few hours, however, of the issuing of this order, information was-brought to Major General Beresford; that Colonel Cambyse, *aide-de-camp* to General Junot, had a seized upon the Prince Regent's horses, had carried them from the royal stables, and was embarking them as the property of General Junot.

The statement, upon being inquired into, was found to be correct, and General Kellerman was applied to, to prevent this robbery; he immediately attacked Colonel Cambyse with great severity of language, and ordered the horses to be restored.

The next day an attempt of the same sort, by the same officer, was made upon one of the carriages belonging to the Duke of Sussex, which was actually embarked; Major General Beresford, upon being made acquainted with it, sent his *aide-de-camp* to Colonel Cambyse, to remonstrate with him (in terms not very agreeable) upon the repetition of a conduct so disgraceful to the character of an officer. This lecture was, however, of but little avail, for, during the time that Major General Berresford's *aide-de-camp* was speaking, the second carriage belonging to the Duke of Sussex was removed to the river, for the same purpose of embarkation; both carriages were afterwards recovered, and Colonel Cambyse threatened with a voyage to England as a prisoner, if he continued a line of conduct such as he had till then pursued. Various other traits might be related of this officer, but an act of General J——'s, will be more interesting, and more worthy of record: he had carried off a considerable number of pictures, and embarked them on board his own vessel, from the house of the Marchioness of Anjija; upon being required to give them up, he answered, that they had been given to him. This having been found to be incorrect, he denied all knowledge of the transaction and impeached a relation of his who was on board the ship with him, but who immediately proceeded to one of the transports, where he hoped to remain concealed. A threat of preventing the General from sailing, till the pictures were disgorged, soon brought this gentleman back to the frigate, and Captain Percy directed him to go on shore to give an account of the transaction; he refused, however, to acknowledge the jurisdiction of the commissioners, and declared his determination not to land. The bayonets of the marines were called for, to persuade him; they proved effectual, the gentleman was landed, and soon after, the pictures were returned. Another general officer, on the day of his embarkation, carried off, from the office of the commissioners, all the papers and documents which he was able to collect, in a short visit he made to it while the commissioners were absent; and if he had not been driven back to Lisbon by contrary winds, (when he was forced to return them) would have involved their proceedings in complete confusion!

On the 10th of September the French garrison evacuated Lisbon, and General Hope was appointed Governor.

The joy of the inhabitants, when the national flag was hoisted, is beyond any description; an universal shout re-echoed through the town; innumerable banners, emblems of a new life of liberty, were displayed, from every corner of the capital. The ships in the river, decorated with the proud symbols of national independence, proclaimed the triumph of the day, by repeated discharges of artillery; and for nine nights the town was universally illuminated, in token of the joy of the inhabitants at their deliverance, and of hatred to the oppressors, who still witnessed. from their transports the detestation which was manifested of them.

Thus was ended the campaign in Portugal. Parts of it are to be regretted, but the great object for which it was undertaken was accomplished. Portugal was freed from the enemy by the genius of Sir Arthur Wellesley, and the bravery of British troops. Those means have preserved it independent, and have since accomplished the deliverance of the Peninsula. The succession of general officers to the command of an army considerably advanced in the operations of a campaign, will rarely be attended with advantage; to cast any blame upon those who succeeded in this instance to the command of the British army in Portugal, would be unjust; but we may be permitted to observe that the genius of a great commander was marked in the first operations of the campaign; whilst a cold calculating policy conducted it to its final issue. Sir Arthur Wellesley soon after embarked for England; Sir Hew Dalrymple and Sir Harry Burrard were recalled; and the British army was entrusted to the command of Sir John Moore.

CHAPTER 4
Corunna

The events of the campaign in Spain had been various, during the period of which; we have been speaking.

When the revolution; first broke out in that country, when the massacre of the 2nd of May had roused every patriot to revenge the murder of his countrymen, the force of the French in Spain was unprepared to repress so universal an insurrection. A corps of 20,000 men was, however, soon despatched, under the orders of General Dupont, to relieve the French fleet at Cadiz, and to seize upon that important post. General Dupont was too late; the Governor Solano, suspected of some attachment to the French, was murdered by the people, and the revolution was organized throughout Andalusia. General Castanos was appointed Captain General, and was invested with the command of all the troops in the south of Spain.

He had a considerable number of veteran regiments, besides the volunteers who had at that time hastened to enrol themselves under the banners of their country. With an army so composed, General Castanos marched to oppose the progress of General Dupont. This officer was waiting, at Cordova and Andujar, the junction of a corps under General Wedel, which was marching to his assistance from Madrid; for although General Dupont had not as yet been opposed by any regular force, yet the universal hostility he had met with from the peasants, as well as the loss he had sustained by their desultory warfare, made it dangerous for him to attempt, a further advance into the country.

General Castanos resolved to meet the French force before it should receive its expected reinforcements; he arrived with rapidity upon the Guadalquivir, opposite Cordova, and advanced upon Andujar. At the same time he detached a considerable corps, under Generals Coupigni and Reding, to pass the river higher up, to place itself in rear of Dupont, and to intercept his communications with Madrid. This object was effected; the corps reached Baylen on the 19th of July, and was placed between the army of Dupont and the,, reinforcement of 6,000: men under General Wedel. General Dupont had on the same evening determined to break up from his position near Andujar, where he had suffered considerably from the hostility of the peasants, as well as from the army of Castanos, which was engaged in continual skirmishes with his troops. He marched during the whole night towards Baylen, and arrived there in the morning; he found, however, the Spanish corps in position to receive him. General Dupont made immediate dispositions for attack; but he was foiled in all his attempts to penetrate the Spanish lines. He expected the arrival of General Wedel; but being at last exhausted, and dreading an attack both in front and rear, (as the corps of Castanos was following him), he sent a flag of truce to the Spaniards about two o'clock in the afternoon, and desired to capitulate. While the terms were discussing, but after some advantages had been seized over General Dupont's army, the corps of General Wedel began to appear in rear of the Spaniards; it soon after made an attack upon them, but was repulsed; and General Dupont was told that unless General Wedel was ordered to desist, and unless his corps was included in the capitulation, the whole of his army would be put to the sword. General Dupont was obliged to agree, and General Wedel was ordered to remain quiet, and to consider his corps as a part of the army which was to surrender. General Wedel feigned obedience to this order, but finding his communication with Madrid was open, he moved off in the course of the night, and endeavoured to reach La Mancha. When his march was discovered, the Spaniards announced to Dupont, that his whole army should pay for the atrocities committed by the French throughout Spain, and be immolated in the morning, unless Wedel was brought back. General Dupont had no means of preventing the execution of so alarming a menace, but complying with the alternative; he sent a senior officer in quest of Wedel, and brought him back from Carolina, which he had already reached: the whole of the two corps laid down their arms the same day, in conformity to a capitulation entered upon for that purpose.

There never was a more singular extinction of an army of near 25,000 men than that which has been described. General Dupont was esteemed the best officer in the French army; yet he surrendered a most effective corps to an army but just formed, and in part composed of inexperienced officers and soldiers. The results were most fortunate for the Spaniards; the kingdoms of Andalusia were freed from enemies, and their armies rendered disposable for the other operations of the war.

About the time that Dupont had been detached to Cadiz, General Moncey had been sent with 8,000 men to reduce Valencia to obedience; he marched for that purpose from Madrid, and arrived without much opposition within sight of the town.

Valencia is an old Moorish capital, surrounded by a very high wall, and secure against a *coup de main*. Moncey determined to attack it; but, without a battering train, he was reduced to the necessity of storming, without having made any preparations for it. The assault was directed against the southern gate, where the Spaniards had placed two guns, and secured them by some works which were not easy to be carried; the troops advanced from one of the streets of the suburbs, along which the Spanish guns did great execution, and at last obliged Moncey to give up the attempt and retire with a considerable diminution of his numbers. The Spanish corps that were without the town menaced his retreat and Moncey was forced to march with great rapidity towards Alcira and St, Philippe, to-secure a passage by a different road from that by which he had entered the kingdom. He was continually harassed, but he succeeded in crossing the river Xucar, and afterwards retired to Madrid with about half the corps he had originally taken from it.

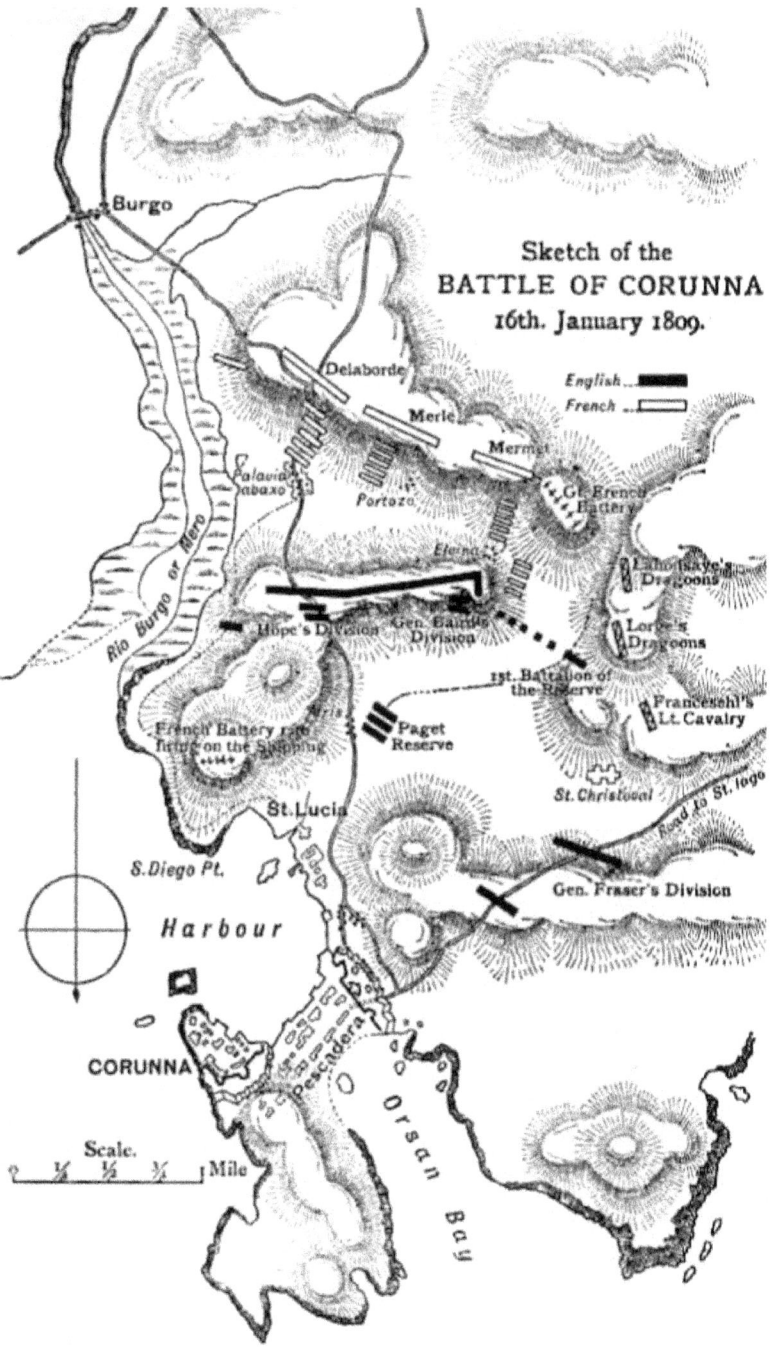

The French were more successful in the battle of Rio Seco, mention of which has already been made in the first pages of this work yet they were unable to follow up their successes; and the noble resistance of Saragossa, under the directions of Palafox, obliged them to march a considerable corps to besiege it.

The events of this campaign were so destructive to the enemy, that Joseph resolved to quit Madrid, and seek a safer and more concentrated position behind the Ebro. The first columns of his troops began to retire from the capital upon the 30th of July, and it was totally abandoned on the 10th of August; the siege of Saragossa was also raised, and the headquarters of the French armies were established at Vittoria. Such was the state of things when Lieutenant General Sir John Moore was ordered to carry the British army from Portugal to the assistance of the Spaniards.

The Spanish troops were generally assembled in two great corps; the left, under the orders of General Blake, in the provinces of Asturias and Biscay; the right, along the south bank of the Ebro, at Logrono, Tudela, &c, and under the command of Castanos; Palafox commanded the army of Arragon; which, (although incorporated with that of Castanos), yet yielded but an unwilling submission to his orders. The Marquis of Romana, with the troops that had been withdrawn from Denmark, had landed in Galicia, and was moving forward to take the chief command of the troops of Blake and the whole northern army.

Sir John Moore began his march from Lisbon on the 27th of October; he determined to assemble his troops at Salamanca; but, from the difficulties of roads, and of subsistence for the army, he was induced to separate his corps, and to march them at distances so great from each other, that they no longer were of any mutual support. The infantry arrived in good order at Salamanca towards the end of November; but the cavalry and artillery, which had moved within a few leagues of Madrid, did not reach that place till three weeks or a month afterwards. Sir David Baird was sent from England with a corps of 13,000 men to Corunna, and was directed to place himself under the orders of Sir John Moore, and effect his junction with him as early as possible. This officer met with considerable obstructions from the Junta of Galicia; he was, in the first instance, refused the permission to land; and afterwards was subjected to great inconvenience in provisioning his troops.

Soon after the arrival of Sir John Moore at Salamanca, he was apprized that Bonaparte, with a large army, was already in Spain; and that his first successes had been considerable; Sir John Moore seemed to think them decisive.

The army of General Blake was beaten at Espinosa de los Monteros on the 10th and 11th of November; and the battle of Tudela on the 28th put to rout the army of Castanos. Sir John Moore had a most difficult card to play. His army was not assembled, his cavalry and artillery had not formed their junction, and a considerable distance divided him from the corps of Sir David Baird. He resolved therefore to abandon offensive operations, and directing this last-mentioned corps to retreat to Vigo, and there embark for Lisbon, he himself prepared to retire into Portugal. The direction of the French army upon Madrid changed, however, Sir John Moore's determination. He stopped the movement of Sir David Baird, and ordered him to advance his corps to Benavente; from whence it was his intention to combine an operation with the whole British force upon the rear of Bonaparte.

General Soult commanded a corps of the French army upon the Carrion; Sir John-Moore determined to attack him, and moved forward with that intention with the whole force under his command, which he had assembled on the 20th of December at Mayorga, combined with the corps of Romana upon his left. The British force amounted to 29,360 effective men. After severe marches, Sir John Moore reached Sahagun on the 21st of December, and prepared on the 23rd to force the position of General Soult. He received, however, information that Bonaparte was marching upon Salamanca, and was seeking to surround his army. Sir John Moore instantly gave up the offensive, and retired in the greatest haste upon Benavente. When he arrived there, he found the advanced guard of Bonaparte's army at a short distance from the place; and on the 29th of December, the British rear guard of cavalry distinguished itself in an affair with the cavalry of the Imperial Guard.

The superiority of the British was manifest on this occasion; they had in several preceding actions given samples of their bravery and good conduct; Lieutenant General Lord Paget and Major General the Honourable C. Stewart had led them on to the most decisive successes, and in an affair at Sahagun, on the 21st of December, had almost annihilated a regiment of French cavalry.

The fall of Madrid, after an inconsiderable resistance, had made a deep impression upon the mind of Sir John Moore; he looked with despondency upon the affairs of the Peninsula, after its surrender; and considered the great cause of Spanish independence completely lost. He had made one effort to relieve the southern provinces of Spain from the eruption with which they were threatened; he succeeded in diverting it against himself; and from that time he conceived that his first duty was to withdraw from the country. With that view he commenced his retreat into Galicia; he at first determined to embark his army at Vigo; he afterwards led it to Corunna. It had been expected that he would have defended the strong ground he was passing over, but he continued his retreat, and once only, on the 8th of January at Lugo, offered battle to his pursuers.[2] The enemy was neither strong enough nor mad enough to accept it; and after a retreat, the most disastrous for an unbeaten but brave and gallant army that history records, Sir John Moore arrived at Corunna on the 11th of January 1809. He took up a position in front of the town to await the arrival of the transports; fortunately they were not long delayed; they reached the harbour on the 14th; and Sir John Moore prepared to embark his troops. Happily for the honour of the British army, though we must lament the loss that ensued, the French were too proud of the reputation they had gained against other armies, to permit

---

2. One of the principal causes of the uninterrupted continuation of this retreat was the total failure of the Commissariat in the establishment of the Magazines which had been directed to be formed on the line of march now pursued by the army.

the embarkation to be unmolested. They attacked the British corps, reduced by fatigue, by loss upon the march, by sickness, and by the absence of its cannon, which was already on board the transports; they attacked it when mustering only 16,000 men, placed in a bad position, with its retreat cut off if beaten; yet they were completely repulsed, with very severe loss, and a part of the position which they occupied before the action, was carried at the point of the bayonet, and maintained. The loss on the side of the British was considerable; Sir John Moore fell in the arms of victory; he died a death worthy of the character he had maintained through a long life of service and renown; he fell by a cannon-shot while directing a charge against the enemy, and commanded the respect, the admiration, and regret of his brother soldiers and his countrymen. Sir David Baird was severely wounded, and obliged to quit the field, and the command devolved upon Sir John Hope. This officer withdrew his troops from the position, and embarked them in the course of the night and succeeding day; the rear-guard was commanded by Major General Beresford, and the whole army was embarked without loss, and sailed on the 17th of January; Thus ended the second campaign in which the British troops had been engaged in the Peninsula. It would be a melancholy task to canvass it throughout; the last action was worthy of the men that have since delivered Spain from its merciless invaders; but the movements which preceded it were far from being generally approved. Great difficulties were indeed opposed to Sir John Moore; but it would appear that in his own mind they were too highly rated. He discharged his duty to his country, however, with his utmost zeal. He died fighting to maintain its glory, and his name will ever be ranked amongst its heroes.

CHAPTER 5
Oporto

During the period of Sir John Moore's campaign in Spain, Sir John Craddock had been appointed to the command of the British troops in Portugal. Their number was small, and varied considerably during the winter; some detachments which had been sent to Sir John Moore returned without having effected their junction, and many stragglers and sick from that army found their way into Portugal, and were formed into battalions. The brigade under Major General R. Stewart was also incorporated with the army under the orders of Sir John Craddock.

Before the retreat of Sir John Moore was known in England, a corps, under the orders of Major General Mackenzie, had been sent to Cadiz, with the view of being admitted as the garrison of that place. The conduct of the Spaniards, in refusing to allow the British army to enter Ferrol, although pressed by a superior enemy, made it necessary. For the Government of England to secure a point of safety for its fleet and armies, before it could consent to the further cooperation of any British force in Spain. It therefore required, as a condition to the employment of an army for the defence of the southern provinces of the Peninsula, that a British force should be admitted within the walls of Cadiz. Much negotiation took place upon this point, but the Spanish Government at last refused the permission, and thus put an end to the proposed assistance of a British army.

The corps under Major General Mackenzie sailed from Cadiz to Lisbon, and added to the force under Sir John Craddock.

After the evacuation of Corunna, by Lieutenant General Sir

John Hope, the French had entered it with two corps, those of Marshals Ney and Soult; the latter was detached, about the beginning of February, to the attack of Portugal. He succeeded, with little opposition, in occupying the country to the north of the Douro. In Oporto, the Portuguese force was collected to a considerable amount; but having neither discipline nor regularity, it was unable: to oppose more than a feeble resistance to the French. Marshal Soult, who was anxious to strike terror amongst the inhabitants of Portugal, permitted his soldiers, after storming the town, and destroying an immense number of people, to continue their cruelties during several days. The plunder of the place was accompanied with every description of outrage; but the measure only succeeded in increasing the detestation in which the enemy was held, without effecting the subjugation of the country.

After the success of Bonaparte in the centre of Spain, and the expulsion of the English army from Galicia, General Victor had been detached against the Spanish corps of General Cuesta, which was quartered about Medellin. After some previous movements a general battle was fought, in which the Spanish army was completely routed; it retired to the mountains about Monasterio, where, with the assistance of the reinforcements which were sent to it, it made head against the French army. Victor at this time concerted with Marshal Soult, in Oporto, a combined attack upon the unconquered provinces of Portugal. Soult was to move through Coimbra, upon Lisbon; while Victor was to cooperate from the Spanish frontier, through Portalegre, or Alcantara, upon Abrantes, and from thence to march upon the capital. Sir John Craddock had collected the British force, which had now become respectable from the different reinforcements which had arrived, in positions in front of Santarem, and upon the road to Coimbra, so as to be prepared to move upon either of the two French corps, which threatened to advance upon him. But on the 22nd of April, Sir Arthur Wellesley (who had been selected for the command in Portugal) arrived with some reinforcements, and assumed the direction of the army.

He decided to proceed instantly against the corps under

Marshal Soult, in Oporto. He left a division under Major General Mackenzie, with the brigade of heavy cavalry under Major General Fane, at Abrantes, to watch the corps of Marshal Victor: some Portuguese were placed to observe the bridge of Alcantara, and with the rest of the army he proceeded to the Douro. By the rapidity of his movement, Sir Arthur Wellesley disconcerted the plans of the French; he drove their advance guard, in three days, from the Vouga to Oporto, and arrived on the Douro, opposite to that town, upon the 11th of May.

Sir Arthur Wellesley had detached Marshal Beresford (who had lately been appointed to the command of the Portuguese army) to pass the Douro, near Lamego, and to occupy Amaranthe; he had also directed General Silviera with the troops under his command, to retain possession of Chaves. By these movements he had hoped to enclose the French corps, in the north of Portugal. On the morning of the 12th he determined to cross the Douro, in face of the enemy, and to attack the town of Oporto, although the bridge had been destroyed, and the boats (with the exception of two that conveyed over the first soldiers) had been removed to the opposite side of the river.

No operation could be more difficult, or require greater bravery in the troops to execute or talent in the general to combine; but complete success attended it. Marshal Soult was surprised; the British army passed the river in spite of every obstacle, and of the superior numbers which were brought to overwhelm the first regiments that crossed; and the French army was driven, with the loss of its sick and wounded, of great part of its baggage, and of a considerable number of guns, from the town of Oporto. Sir Arthur Wellesley pursued the French on the following day; Marshal Beresford had driven them from Amaranthe; so that, being pressed on all sides, they were obliged to abandon the whole of their guns and baggage, and to fly the country by the mountain roads to Orense; their rear was several times attacked, but the main body could not be attained; and Sir Arthur Wellesley, unable any longer to pursue an enemy who had abandoned everything which constitutes an army, and who fled without artillery, baggage, or equipment, halted on the 18th at Monte Alegre, and gave up the pursuit.

This short campaign, of only ten days, is perhaps the most brilliant that ever has been executed. Marshal Soult, represented as the best officer in the French army, had occupied the northern provinces of Portugal, for upwards of two months; he had contemplated the entire conquest of the country, and was employed in organizing the necessary means. To defend himself from any attack, he had the Vouga, and the Douro, both formidable rivers, and the advantage of the strongest country in the Peninsula; he had a force equal in amount to the British, or within very little of it, and in a state of superior military organization. He had a perfect knowledge of the country; he commanded its resources; and was in every way formidable from his talents and his means. Yet the genius of Sir Arthur Wellesley deprived him at once of the advantages of which he was possessed. In the space of four days he was driven from Coimbra to the Douro; and in six days after, not having had the time or opportunity of defending himself in a single position, he was chased from the frontiers of Portugal.

The movements of the Portuguese about Chaves had disappointed the expectations of Sir Arthur Wellesley, or his triumph would have been more complete. He had entertained the hope of surrounding the French army; but by the non-execution of a part of his plan the individuals who composed it escaped; but there never was a more disgraceful escape; or a retreat (if it deserve that name, and not a flight) more humiliating to the officer who conducted it.

Lieutenant General Paget, who had displayed the greatest talent and bravery in the attacks he conducted, with the advanced guard under his command, before his arrival upon the Douro, passed that river with the first company of the Buffs; and having most gallantly sustained, the desperate attack of the enemy upon the few troops under his orders, which had as yet arrived upon the Oporto side of the river; was unfortunately wounded in the arm, and suffered amputation. Major Hervey also lost his arm, in a most gallant charge of the 14th Light Dragoons, which he had led.

Whilst Sir Arthur Wellesley had been engaged in the pursuit of Marshal Soult, Marshal Victor had made a movement upon the bridge of Alcantara, and had threatened to enter Portugal in that direction; the bridge was destroyed, and Marshal Victor made no further advance; but Sir Arthur Wellesley, after making the necessary dispositions for the security of the northern frontiers of Portugal, brought back his army to the Tagus. The state of the French in the Peninsula, at this moment, was as follows. Marshal Ney was at Corunna, Soult was retreating from Portugal, and Mortier was at Valladolid; these corps together amounted to about 60,000 effective men, and kept the provinces of Galicia, Asturias, Biscay, and Castile, in tolerable subjection. There were other corps employed in those provinces, but the amount of force of which we have spoken, was to a certain degree disposable. In the centre of Spain, Victor was at Merida; Sebastiani in La Mancha; and Joseph, with Jourdan, at Madrid; their force amounted to 50,000 men; Suchet was at Saragossa, in occupation of Arragon, with a corps of 20,000 men. The French force in Catalonia was considerable, but, from the state of that province, it could not be disposable for any offensive operations.

The distribution of the Spanish force was, General Cuesta at Monasterio, with 40,000 men, mostly recruits; Vanegas, with 25,000 in the Carolina; Romana, with 25,000 in different parts of Galicia; and General Blake, with 20,000 in Valencia. There were several other corps in different quarters, of small amount, but which could not be considered as efficient for the duties of a campaign. In Portugal, the army of Sir Arthur Wellesley consisted of about 22,000 effective infantry, and 2,500 cavalry. The Portuguese, under Marshal Beresford, were as yet backward in organization, but amounted to about 15,000 men, collected and ready to take the field; besides the troops in garrisons, depots, &c. According to this estimate, the French had a force of 130,000 effective men, while that opposed to them was about 150,000.

CHAPTER 6

Talavera

Sir Arthur Wellesley, upon his arrival on the Tagus, determined, if possible, to liberate Madrid. To effect this object, he proposed to bring the greater part of his own force, with that under General Cuesta, and the corps under General Vanegas, amounting in the whole to near 90,000 men, to operate upon the forces of Joseph, Victor, and Sebastiani, estimated at 50,000. He proposed to leave Marshal Beresford, in conjunction with the Duke del Parque, to watch Soult, from the neighbourhood of Ciudad Rodrigo; and he hoped that the troops under Romana would give sufficient employment to Marshal Ney, in Galicia.

During the month of June Victor (in consequence of the successful operations of Sir Arthur Wellesley against Soult, and his return upon the Tagus) withdrew his corps from the neighbourhood of Monasterio, crossed the Tagus at the bridge of Almaraz, and took up a position at Talavera de la Reyna; General Cuesta followed him to that place, but finding him in position, retired to Almaraz, where he remained, with his advance corps, under the Duke of Albuquerque, at Arzobispo. Towards the end of the same month, Marshal Soult arrived with the corps under his command, at Puebla di Senabria, from whence he marched to Zamora and Salamanca.

In this state of things, Sir Arthur Wellesley (after having received the most distinct declarations from the supreme Government of Spain that his army should be supplied with provisions) advanced on the 25th and 26th of June, from Abrantes, towards Placencia. Marshal Beresford moved at the same time to the neighbourhood of Ciudad Rodrigo. Sir Arthur Wellesley went on the 12th to the headquarters of General Guesta, at Casas del Puerta, near the bridge of Almaraz, to concert with him the operations of the campaign. He proposed as the first object, to occupy in strength the positions of Banos and Bejar, which commanded the only road from Upper Castile into Estramadura, and the country about Coria, and Placencia. Sir Arthur Wellesley (aware that his own army was the only one that was efficient for the operations of a campaign) recommended that a corps of Spaniards should be destined for this service.

It has since been known, that amongst the numberless intriguers who at this moment sought to disunite the counsels of the allies, one of the most busy had awakened the jealousy of General Cuesta upon this point, and had represented to him, that the English general, with a view of weakening the Spanish force in the field, would recommend him to make a considerable detachment from his army. When the recommendation was given, therefore, General Cuesta was convinced that the information he had received was correct; and from the violence of his own nature, could not easily repress his resentment at a proposal, which he thought was intended to reduce his army, for the purpose of diminishing his share of glory in the expulsion of the French from Madrid; a result which he anticipated from the movements about to be carried into execution. General O'Donaju, the adjutant-general of the Spanish army, prevailed upon him, however, to agree to the arrangement, but General Cuesta never carried it fairly into effect. The small force he afterwards sent to Bejar was incompetent to any resistance, and was totally unprovided, even with ammunition.

The remainder of Sir Arthur Wellesley's plan was, that his army should join that of General Cuesta, and should advance in the first instance to the attack of Victor at Talavera; by a movement in cooperation, General Vanegas was ordered to break up from the position in La Mancha, about Madrilejos; to march upon Pembleque and Ocaña, and pass the Tagus at Fuente Dueñas; where he was to arrive on the same day, the 22nd of July, that the armies under Sir Arthur Wellesley and General Cuesta, were to arrive at Talavera, and attack the corps of Victor. General Vanegas received this order, and agreed to its execution. Sir Arthur Wellesley removed his army from Placencia, according to the plan which had been arranged; passed the Tietar, and arrived at Oropesa on the 20th of July; where he effected his junction with the army under the orders of General Cuesta, amounting to 35,000 effective men. The next day, the Spanish army advanced towards Talavera; and on the 22nd the British corps moved forward to the same place. While upon his march, Sir Arthur Wellesley received several messages from General Cuesta, stating that the enemy was disposed to attack him. Sir Arthur Wellesley pushed forward, but upon reaching the ground, found only two squadrons of French, who had come from Talavera to reconnoitre the position of the Spaniards.

The light troops of both armies advanced upon the rearguard of the French, the Spanish cavalry attempted to charge it, but without effect, and the whole French army took up a position upon the heights, to the eastward of the Alberche. The British and Spanish armies occupied the ground about Talavera with their advance upon the right of the same river. Sir Arthur Wellesley had expected to hear from General Vanegas: according to the orders which had been sent to him, he should have been at Fuente Dueñas upon the 22nd; but from every information which could be obtained, no movement appeared to have been made by him. The history of the defection of his corps deserves to be recorded. When General Vanegas received the orders from General Cuesta to move upon Madrid, he returned for answer, that he would do so; he despatched, however, at the same time, a courier to the supreme Junta, communicating to it the orders he had received. That body replied, that he was not to execute the movement, but to await its further commands in the positions which he occupied. These directions (which were neither announced to Sir Arthur Wellesley nor to General Cuesta) arrived in time to stop General Vanegas. It was difficult to explain the motive of this conduct; but it was afterwards discovered that the supreme Junta, amongst other reasons, was not anxious that General Cuesta should enter Madrid. He was supposed to entertain sentiments hostile to many of those who composed it, and not friendly, to the whole body; the Junta, therefore, feared, that if he reached Madrid, he would effect a counter-revolution, and place himself at the head of the government; or at least overturn the Junta's power. This explanation of its motive gained considerable weight from the conduct of that body, when it received General Cuesta's despatches, stating that he had formed his junction with Sir Arthur Wellesley at Oropesa, and was proceeding to Madrid. The Junta then, with as much alacrity as it had sent counter-orders before, directed General Vanegas to move forward, and constituted him captain-general of the province of Madrid; so that, upon his arrival there, he would be superior to General Cuesta, under whose orders up to that moment he had been placed. Although by this conduct the general effect of the plan proposed by Sir Arthur Wellesley was destroyed, yet he resolved to attack the corps of Marshal Victor, and on the morning of the 23rd moved his columns for that purpose into a wood close to the Alberche, and stretching along the right of the French army.

The plan of the movement which he determined upon, was to cross the river, attack the right of Marshal Victor with the whole of the British infantry, move the whole cavalry upon the centre of the enemy, and engage their left with the Spanish infantry.

The corps of Marshal Victor was 22,000 men; the allied army was 50,000. The troops of which it was composed were not all of equally good materials; but the number of English only would almost have secured success if the attack had taken place. General Cuesta, however, refused to march till the following morning; and Sir Arthur Wellesley with considerable reluctance was constrained to yield to his determination. Some alterations were made in the course of the night in the disposition of the troops. General Bassecour, with a Spanish division, was ordered to the left of the British, and was to have passed the Alberche in the rear of the enemy. Sir R. Wilson, who commanded a corps

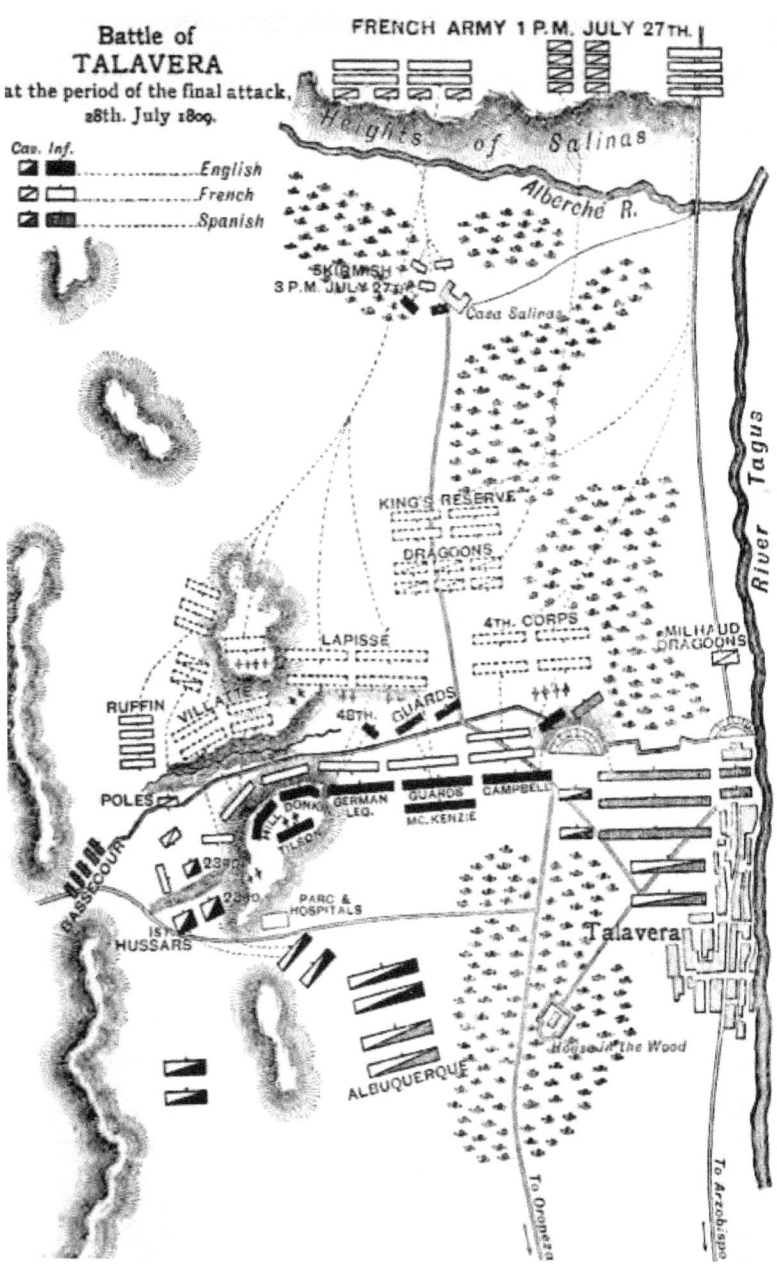

of light troops, Spanish and Portuguese, was also ordered still further along the banks of the Alberche to Escalona.

Marshal Victor, however, got information of the intended attack, and retired from his position in the night. Nothing could have been more unfortunate for the allied army; infinitely superior in numbers, it was at the point of making a combined attack upon him, from which it would seem almost impossible he should have escaped without considerable loss; by his retreat unhurt, the nature of the campaign was changed, and the bright prospects of the allies destroyed.

Sir Arthur Wellesley, since his arrival at Talavera, had complained of the total failure on the part of the Spaniards in the supply of his army with provisions. The necessities of the British troops made it impossible to advance; and after the retreat of the French army, Sir Arthur Wellesley was compelled to remain at Talavera till supplies should arrive to him: but recommended the Spaniards, who had not the same deficiencies, to move upon Cavalla, upon the road to Toledo, and endeavour to communicate with General Vanegas, who was still supposed to have made some movement in La Mancha. General Cuesta, however, without communicating with Sir Arthur Wellesley, took the road to Sta. Olalla, where he arrived with the whole Spanish army on the morning of the 25th. From this place he gave notice of the defection of the corps of Vanegas.

On the morning of the 26th General Cuesta's advance was attacked by the advanced guard of the French army. It appeared that Joseph had called General Sebastiani from La Mancha to Toledo; that with all the force he could withdraw from Madrid, he had marched himself to join him; and that he had formed a junction with these two corps and the corps of General Victor, at or near Torrijos; that he had immediately advanced upon General Cuesta; and was in hopes of beating him before he should be joined by the British. General Cuesta, however, upon learning the force of the enemy, retired to Talavera. Sir Arthur Wellesley had endeavoured to find a situation in which to fight a battle in front of the, Alberche, but not having succeeded, determined to take up a position, the right upon the town of Talavera, the left upon some heights, about a mile to the northward of it. The Spanish army retired during the 26th and 27th, and took up the ground marked out for it about the town of Talavera. On the morning of the 27th Sir Arthur Wellesley sent a brigade of cavalry and two brigades of infantry, the whole under the orders of Major General Mackenzie, to watch the enemy upon the left of the Alberche, and to protect the retreat of the Spaniards.

Towards two o'clock in the afternoon the French advance of cavalry began to skirmish with the British. Major General Mackenzie soon after retired, and about four-o'clock passed the Alberche with the whole of his corps. He took up a position in a wood upon the right bank of it, from which he could observe the movements of the enemy.

Joseph had brought the whole of his army to the opposite side of the river; and believing (from the small number of troops that were to be seen upon the right bank) that the allies were retreating, he determined to push in their advanced guard immediately, with the hope of falling upon their army on its march to the bridge of Almaraz; to which place alone, after abandoning the line of the Alberche, he thought it could be retiring. The French infantry passed the river the brigade of Colonel Donkin, which was posted to defend it, was to a certain degree surprised. The river was fordable at all points, and the-French advanced guard fell upon this brigade and caused it considerable loss. Sir Arthur Wellesley (who had just arrived upon the ground) ordered the whole of Major General Mackenzie's division to retire from the wood, and to fall back upon the position in the rear, into which the army was at this time moving.

The French, elated with their first, successes, pushed forward as rapidly as the passage of their troops would allow, and threw their right forward, with the view of turning the town of Talavera. The Duke of Albuquerque showed, however, so good a front with the cavalry under his orders (which was in a plain upon the left of the British) that this movement was considerably delayed. Sir Arthur Wellesley was tempted (while a part only of the French army had passed the Alberche) to attack it with the whole of the allies; but upon considering the lateness of the hour, he continued his movement to the position he had fixed upon. The British advanced guard retired under cover of the cavalry, and took up the ground allotted to it. The French continued to press forward; and, at last, when it was nearly dark, brought a battery of six guns, supported by a considerable corps of infantry, to some high ground opposite the height upon which the left of the British was to rest. The troops destined for this point had not at that moment reached it. Colonel Donkin's brigade, which was, retiring near it, was ordered to form at the foot of the hill upon the left of the Germans under General Sherbrooke. But the French, supported by their guns, attacked these corps, drove them from the ground they occupied, and carried the height. Lieutenant General Hill's and Major General R. Stewart's brigades were at that moment ascending it from the other side; their advance found the French upon the top. The battalion of detachments under Colonel Bunbury wheeled into line, charged, and retook the hill. The French, however, returned to the attack, but were finally driven to the foot of it. The action upon this point was severe; Major General Hill was at one moment mixed with the French soldiers; several men of both armies were killed or wounded with the bayonet, but the gallantry of British soldiers, and the intrepidity of their officers, prevailed.

During this attack, the Spanish troops were alarmed by the fire of the French, who were following the British cavalry in its retreat through the centre of the allies; they immediately began a fire which was taken up by the whole of the first line. Several of the officers of the Guards who were standing in front of their men, and many of the light troops of the Germans who were posted in, advance, were killed or wounded by this fire. The French, however, were checked by it, and remained without making any further attack during the night. It appeared afterwards that the French officers discovered that the whole army was in front of Talavera, only from the firing which has just been described; they were ignorant of any position about that town, and, therefore, till then, had given out to their soldiers that the allied army was retiring.

At daybreak on the 28th the French recommenced their attack with 14,000 men, by assaulting the hill from which they had been driven the-night before. Their troops had been collected during dark, and were formed at the bottom of the height; they moved at a signal given, and succeeded in ascending to a considerable distance before they were checked the fire of the British. From the conical shape of this hill it was difficult to form any considerable number of men to defend it: but the regiments which were on it charged the French troops with an impetuosity they were unable to resist, and drove them, with considerable loss and in total confusion, beyond the ground from which they had moved to the attack.

The British cavalry had been ordered up to charge the French fight as they were retiring, but unfortunately it was at too great a distance to effect this object.

After the failure of this attempt upon the hill, the French continued to cannonade the British line for a considerable time; but the fire ceased at length on both sides, and perfect tranquillity reigned throughout the opposing armies. During this interval, Sir Arthur Wellesley communicated with General Cuesta near a house in the centre of the lines, and afterwards slept, till some fresh movements in the enemy's camp were reported to him.

Joseph having been defeated in the several efforts he had made upon the British left, determined to try his fortune upon the centre of the allied army. The attack which followed was made under cover of a wood of olives, and fell principally upon the brigade commanded by Major General Alexander Campbell; this officer had. taken advantage of some high banks which intersected the ground he occupied, and through the means of which he. was enabled, with a very inferior force, to arrest the progress of the enemy's principal column. Being at one time, however, driven from one of these banks, he rallied the regiment which was retiring, charged the column which was pursuing him, drove it from the ground of which it had taken possession, and took twelve pieces, of artillery; at the same time some squadrons of the Spanish regiment of cavalry of the King, charged the head of a French column of infantry which was advancing through the wood, in pursuit of some Spanish infantry that had given way, and cut up a considerable part of it. Thus terminated the second attack of the memorable 28th of July; the enemy was completely repulsed, with the loss of seventeen pieces of artillery upon different points, and a very considerable number of his best troops. His failures seemed decisive of the day; another pause ensued, considerable movements on the part of the enemy were observed, and for some time were construed by the allied army as indicative of a retreat; but the severest action was yet to come.

The whole *état major* of the French was observed to have collected in front of the left of the British; after some consultation amongst the officers who composed it, they appeared to have decided upon a new arrangement of their army. The *aides-de-camp* were despatched in different directions, and soon after the French divisions were observed to be moving to their new destinations. It now seemed to be the intention of the enemy to bring the great body of, his force to act upon that part of the British line which was occupied by the Guards; and, at the same time, to move with three columns of infantry and a regiment of cavalry, along the valley which extended under the height which formed the left of the British line. These columns were supported by some light infantry, which the enemy had thrown upon the chain of hills which run westward beyond the valley, and which were destined to turn the British left and attack it upon the flank and rear.

To meet this movement Sir Arthur Wellesley directed the cavalry (which was concealed in the valley) to be prepared to charge the columns of infantry, as soon as they should have extended their formation, and exposed their flank. He also directed the guards to be prepared for the attack which was going to be made upon them, and upon no account to move from the ground they occupied.

The French columns of infantry which had moved into the valley, were more advanced than those destined for the attack upon the Guards; they had halted near a house within gun-shot of the British left, and appeared to be waiting for orders to advance. Major General Payne, who commanded the British cavalry, seized this opportunity to attack them; the enemy, observing the forward movement of the cavalry, formed himself against the side of this house in solid column; he had a deep ravine, or water-course, along his front, of which the British cavalry was not aware, and he was besides supported by sixteen guns. The charge of the cavalry was thrown into confusion by this ravine; many of the horses fell into it; and the portion which got over it was so divided and broken as a body, that the effect of the charge was completely done away. The bravery of the British soldier was not, however, to be daunted by this check. The Honourable Major Ponsonby led the men who were near him upon the bayonets of the enemy; but their valour could not compensate for the total confusion into which they had been thrown. The bravery of individuals could effect nothing against a solid body of infantry; the soldiers who were repulsed by the French columns galloped forward upon the regiment of cavalry which supported them, and in a short time the whole plain was covered with British dragoons dispersed in all directions, and totally without formation. In this state they were charged by some French regiments which were in reserve; many of them were taken, the remainder, passed through the intervals in the French columns, and those that escaped their fire, of whom Lord William Russell was one, retired within the British lines.

In this attack the 23rd Light Dragoons lost two-thirds of its number; its charge was injudicious; the ground in front had not been reconnoitred, and the French infantry was too strongly posted to promise it success. The order for the cavalry was to charge when the French columns had extended and exposed their flank. They had done neither when the attack was made, but the bravery with which it was conducted, put an end to the movements which the enemy had intended on that side; and he never stirred afterwards from the ground upon which he was formed.

Sir Arthur Wellesley observed this hesitation and profited by it, in detaching the 48th Regiment, which he had called for the defence of the height when it was threatened with an attack, to support the movement which the guards had at this moment made upon the enemy. These troops, with a part of Major General Cameron's brigade, had been attacked by the whole reserve of the French army; but they had received it with so tremendous a fire, that they forced it to give way; charged it with great impetuosity and pursued it into a wood. They had not proceeded to any great distance, however, when the enemy brought so considerable a number of guns to bear upon their flank, that in a very few moments all their mounted officers were killed or wounded and near 500 of their men. In this situation the Guards were forced to fall back in considerable confusion: they passed through the intervals of the 48th Regiment, which had just arrived, to support them, and which checked the advance of the enemy. The attack was most severe upon this regiment; it maintained its ground in the most gallant manner, till the guards had re-formed, and moved forward to its support. When the French perceived these troops advancing, they retired; the Guards instantly huzza'd; the cry was echoed along the whole line; the enemy continued their retreat and thus ended the last achievement of the battle of Talavera. The enemy was soon perceived to be moving to the rear; he showed a considerable force of cavalry, and maintained a heavy cannonade to cover the retreat; and at the close of the day he had already passed a portion of his troops across the Alberche.

There never was a more extraordinary battle than the one which has now been described: the French brought into the field a force of not less than 47,000 men, and the whole of their attacks, with the most trifling exception, were directed against the British army, not exceeding 18,000 infantry, and 1,500 cavalry. Yet the British general had nerve to maintain the contest, and ability to baffle the efforts of the enemy. The army displayed a courage and perseverance, which did justice to the confidence with which its commander had relied upon it; and proved to Spain and to the world, what the dauntless spirit of the British soldier is capable of effecting, when under the direction of such an officer.

The enemy did justice to the talent of Sir Arthur Wellesley, and to the unrivalled bravery of his troops;. Marshal Victor admitted to an English officer who was taken prisoner, that much as he had heard of the gallantry of English soldiers, still he could not have believed that any men could have been led to attacks so desperate as some that he had witnessed in the battle of Talavera. The glory of the British arms shone forth, in brighter colours on this memorable day than it had ever done amidst its countless triumphs of years preceding. The soldiers struggled against privations of every description; as well as against a force which seemed calculated to overwhelm them; their native valour spurred them on to conquest, and stifled every feeling which could arrest or make it doubtful.

On the morning of the 29th, the light division of 3,000 men, under Major General Crawford, joined the army from Oropesa; it was immediately ordered to form the advance, and take up a position in the front of the field of battle. The allies were employed in attending their wounded, and burying or burning the dead of both armies.

The British loss was 5,000 men in killed or wounded; the loss of the Spaniards was much inferior. The French loss was estimated by themselves at 14,000 men, Joseph retired in the course of the 29th with the greatest part of his army, to Sta. Olalla; a rear guard of 6,000 men was left at Casas Leguas to cover his retreat, but it retired on the night of the 30th, and joined the corps to which it belonged near Toledo.

CHAPTER 7
Almonacid

The army of General Vanegas, which had advanced from Madrilejos, in obedience to the orders of the supreme Junta, had arrived upon the Tagus, near Aranjuez and Toledo on the 28th. The advance of his corps pushed on in the night to within a short distance of Madrid, and took some patrols which had been sent out from the garrison; but General Vanegas having heard that the French army was retreating towards the capital from the field of Talavera, recalled the parties that had crossed the Tagus, and abandoned any further offensive operations. Sir Arthur Wellesley, who was still unable to advance—from the total want of provisions in which the Spaniards kept him, recommended to General Cuesta to form a junction with General Vanegas; but while this movement was in contemplation, information was brought from Placencia, that the, corps of Soult was moving upon that town, and that the troops at Bejar, hearing of its advance; had abandoned that position, and left the road open to its march. Sir Arthur Wellesley could hardly believe that the strong positions about Bejar had been so hastily given up; the corps of Marshal Beresford was ready to have assisted the troops in occupation of them, and a brigade of British, under the orders of Major General Catling Crawford, was within a few days' march, and would have assisted in their defence. But the intelligence being soon after confirmed, Sir Arthur Wellesley decided to carry the British army to attack, General Soult and proposed to General Cuesta to remain in the position of Talavera, to cover the movement of the English upon Placencia. Sir Arthur Wellesley also proposed to leave his wounded in charge of General Cuesta, to whose kindness and generosity he entrusted them, with a solemn promise from him, that if anything should oblige the Spanish army to retire, his first care should be, to move the British to a place of safety. General Cuesta was delighted with the plan which was proposed to him. He felt that his own army was unequal to any contest with the French in an open plain, and that it must be to the British only, that he could look for the expulsion of the enemy from his rear; he also expressed himself most particularly gratified by the confidence which Sir Arthur Wellesley reposed in him, entrusting the wounded to his care.

The necessary arrangements being made, and Major General Mackinnon placed in the command of the hospitals at Talavera, Sir Arthur Wellesley marched on the morning of the 3rd of August for Oropesa. A short time after his arrival at that place, he learnt that the advanced guard of Soult's army was arrived at Naval Moral, and that the Spaniards, who had retired from Bejar, had crossed the Tagus at Almaraz, and destroyed the bridge; he determined, however, to move upon the French, and was in hopes of finding them the following day. General Bassecour, with a Spanish division, was moving along the Tietar, and was destined to act upon the left and rear of the French. About four o'clock in the afternoon, however, a despatch arrived from General Cuesta, announcing to Sir Arthur Wellesley, that, from intelligence upon which he could rely, he was persuaded that the corps of Marshal Ney had evacuated Galicia, and formed a junction with the corps of Marshal Mortier, from Valladolid; that the two were united with Marshal Soult; and that the amount of the collected force upon the rear of the allied army, could not be less than 55,000 men; that Marshal Victor was at no great distance from Talavera, upon the other side; that he (General Cuesta) apprehended an attack from him and had in consequence determined to break up immediately from that town, and join Sir Arthur Wellesley at Oropesa. This information was as disastrous as it was unexpected: the letter from General Cuesta further stated, that his movement was already begun, and that his army

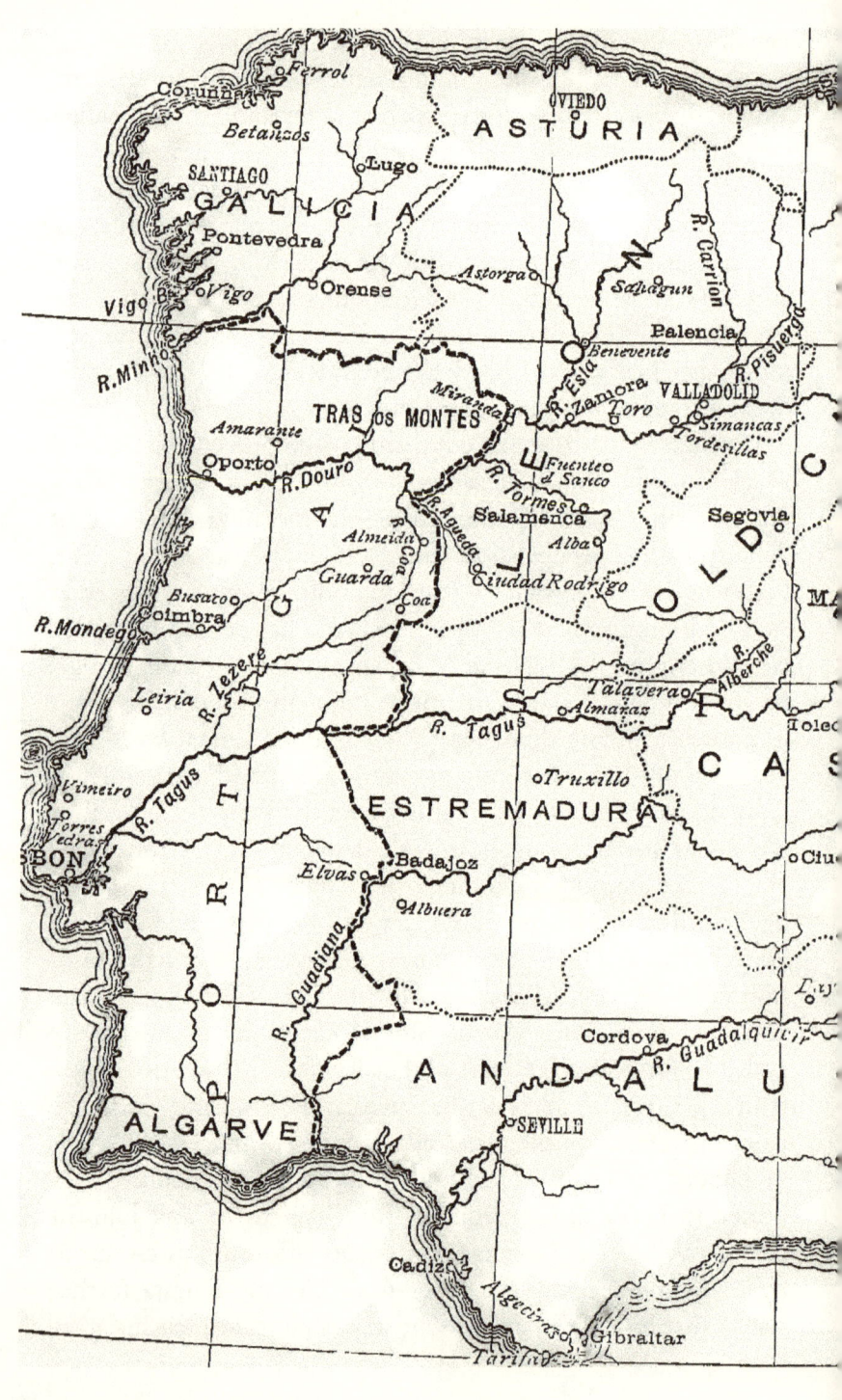

would form its junction with the British in the course of the night: there remained, therefore, no hope of preventing or delaying it, and the whole plan, upon which Sir Arthur Wellesley had undertaken his operation, was at once destroyed.

The bridge of Almaraz was no longer in existence; the bridge of Arzobispo was exposed, by the abandonment of Talavera to the corps of Victor, and the whole allied army, if it advanced, might be cut off from any retreat across the Tagus, while its movement upon Portugal must depend upon the success of its attack upon the combined army of Ney, Soult, and Mortier. In this situation of affairs Sir Arthur Wellesley did not hesitate to give up offensive operations, and retire across the Tagus, by the bridge of Arzobispo.

Sir Arthur Wellesley had every reason to complain of the conduct of General Cuesta; he had abandoned the position entrusted to him, without any ground for so doing; for it afterwards appeared that Victor was at some distance from Talavera, and not occupied in a movement upon the corps of General Cuesta; but, at any rate, the Spaniards evacuated the post entrusted to them, and abandoned the British wounded, with a precipitancy that nothing but the actual presence of an enemy could justify. If General Cuesta was actuated by a desire of bringing his army to the assistance of Sir Arthur Wellesley, who was about to attack a force which he had reason to believe was superior to him, he ought to have waited a few hours, till he had communicated with him, and in the meantime, he should have given assistance to the removal of the British wounded. If he thought that the return of a messenger from Oropesa (a distance of only five leagues), would have exposed him by too much delay, he ought at least to have left a corps to check the enemy in his front, and to have protected the retreat of the hospitals. And, last of all, it was his duty, to which he had also pledged himself in the most solemn manner, to have given all the means in his power to facilitate the removal of the British wounded. He did, however, the direct reverse: he abandoned his position with his whole army, without communication with Sir Arthur Wellesley, indeed, he precluded the possibility of any, by stating in his letter that his army was in march, and to the wounded, instead of every assistance he could command, he gave but *four carts,* for the whole 4,000 men. It is impossible to conceive, that the importance of the occupation of Talavera, to the movement of Sir Arthur Wellesley, should have escaped the observation of General Cuesta: the ground about that town afforded only situation in which the advance of the French army upon the rear of the British, while moving upon Soult, could possibly be resisted; the rest of the country was plain, and offered no defensive position; so that in abandoning it, General Cuesta exposed the whole allied army to an attack, in front and rear. In short, it is very difficult to discover a sound or equitable reason for the precipitancy with which this movement was executed; but the total disregard which was shown to the British wounded, the paltry number of four carts which was afforded them, by an army that was provided with them to excess, remains a stain upon the character of General Cuesta that no time will ever efface.

Sir Arthur Wellesley moved his army, upon the morning of the 4th of August, to the bridge of Arzobispo; the nature of the campaign was changed; Galicia was delivered from the French and the corps of Romana was now in peaceable possession of it, with the opportunity of augmenting its own numbers, and improving its discipline; the whole province was in a situation to dispose of its military means, and to create, in a short time, a powerful diversion upon the rear of the enemy assembled upon the Tagus. The north of Spain was almost entirely in the same situation as Galicia. The French had abandoned it, with very few exceptions, to concentrate their force against the British army and Sir Arthur Wellesley conceived, that although he had been foiled in his attempt to rescue Madrid, yet he had restored independence to Galicia, and in great part to the provinces adjoining it; which might, in the end, prove most advantageous to the cause of Spain. This opinion has since been proved to be correct; Galicia retained its freedom, and the other northern provinces were never afterwards but in partial subjection to the enemy.

As soon as Sir Arthur Wellesley had crossed the Tagus at Arzobispo, he detached Major General Crawford, with the Light Division, to occupy, with as much rapidity as possible, the pass at Almaraz; where it was to be feared the enemy, whose advanced guard had seen the passage of the allies at Arzobispo, might push a force across the Tagus, and endeavour to intercept the British army on its march upon Deleytosa. Major General Crawford arrived, however, in time to prevent that operation; the movement of the army was undisturbed; General Cuesta remained at Arzobispo and the British moved to Deleytosa. The Spaniards were, however, attacked a few days after by the French at Arzobispo; their advanced guard was driven from the bridge; and their whole army retired to Deleytosa, whilst Sir Arthur Wellesley moved to Jaraseco.

The force under General Vanegas had remained since the battle of Talavera, in the neighbourhood of Toledo, but to the southward of the Tagus. General Cuesta was in communication with it, and apprized Vanegas of his retreat from Arzobispo. He directed him in consequence to fall back to the positions about Madrilejos, from which he had originally moved, and upon no account to risk an action with the enemy, but to keep his corps ready to make any movement, in cooperation with the allied army, that might afterwards be determined upon. General Vanegas prepared to carry these orders into execution, and retired a considerable distance through La Mancha; but, from a fatality which has never been explained, he was induced to move forward again, over some of the ground which he had passed, and to engage his corps in a general action with the French under Sebastiani, at Almonacid. The Spaniards were completely routed in this battle; their best troops were engaged in it, and many of the corps behaved with great gallantry and good conduct; but they, were defeated with considerable loss, and were driven to the Sierra Morena. This disaster was severely felt; the dispersion of the troops that could be most depended upon, and who were entrusted with the defence of the great pass into Andalusia, was an event that could not easily be repaired and, in addition, it destroyed all confidence in the movements of the Spaniards; they were no longer to be depended upon, for the most trifling operations: when they were required to act, they remained unmoved; when entrusted with a position, as at Talavera, they deserted it without reason; when directed to avoid an action, which, if successful, could be of no benefit to their cause, they seemed to court one; and when engaged, exposed themselves to the most disastrous defeats. With this battle terminated the campaign, which had been undertaken for the relief of Madrid, and the expulsion of the enemy from the central provinces of Spain. The corps under Sir Robert Wilson retired through the mountains from Escalona to Bejar, where it was attacked and routed by the advanced guard of Marshal Ney, who was returning from the Tagus to the neighbourhood of Salamanca.

CHAPTER 8
Ocaña

Sir Arthur Wellesley remained at Jaraseco, till the French, who had collected upon the Tagus, had dispersed their corps; and till the total failure of supplies obliged him to retire to the frontiers of Portugal, from whence alone he could secure the provisioning of his army.

He placed his headquarters at Badajoz, his advance at Merida, and the rest of his army in cantonments, upon the frontiers of Spain and Portugal. The supreme government of Spain was thrown into considerable consternation by this movement, of which it had been the sole and entire cause. The individuals who composed it sought, notwithstanding, to throw the blame from themselves, upon those who had the most materially suffered by their misconduct.

The Marquis Wellesley, who was at this time the British representative in Spain, complained most bitterly of their inattention and neglect to an army, which had so valiantly fought in their defence; and whose blood had been so profusely spilt, in supporting-the great cause in which they were engaged; but these complaints were only too ably urged. The Spaniards, proud of their former glories, can but ill brook the interference of foreign powers; their pride and haughty independence prompt them to spurn the assistance or control of foreigners and when their government was justly accused of neglect, and even treason to Spain herself, yet as that reproach was from a foreign hand, they rallied round that government, and repelled the accusations, by the most idle and unfounded attacks upon those who made them, and who had full reason to complain of their unjust and unfriendly conduct. A spirit of hostility was thus raised between the allied nations, and for some time there was much of that unpleasant feeling which is generated by mutual accusations. The magnanimous conduct of the British government, however, soon set those jealousies at rest, and by degrees acquired for itself the unbounded confidence of the Spanish nation.

The supreme government of Spain had displaced General Cuesta from the command of his army, during the time that Sir Arthur Wellesley, (now become Lord Wellington) remained at Jaraseco, and General Eguia was entrusted with that important situation. This officer was soon after directed to move the Spanish army, leaving only the Duke of Albuquerque with a small corps in Estremadura, and to form a junction with General Vanegas, in the Sierra Morena, and in the neighbourhood of La Carolina. This operation was dictated, in no small degree, by a feeling of jealousy towards the English. The Spaniards wished to keep their army separate from the British, because they believed it could be rendered more subservient to their own views. While it remained in presence of so distinguished an officer as Lord Wellington, it was curbed, and restrained in' the movements it might be directed to undertake; his advice must necessarily be listened to, and it is not too much to say, that some of the rulers of the country were not at that time unwilling to see their armies directed by weaker counsels than such as would be derived from him.

There was another reason for the movement of that army. It was believed, by many persons in the direction of affairs in Spain, that Lord Wellington was determined to evacuate the country, and retire into Portugal; they thought, however, that by removing the Spanish army from Estremadura, they should shift the defence of that province upon the shoulders of Lord Wellington; by which means, they flattered themselves, they should retain him against his will. Lord Wellington was not so easily to be overreached: he stated to the Spanish government, that he should remain at Badajoz so long as he felt he could be serviceable, to its cause, but without neglecting the first object which he was directed to attend to; namely, the defence of Portugal. He pressed the government to make such arrangements as would secure the provisioning of his army, if he was enabled again to take the field; but above all, he recommended it to preserve the Spanish armies from being harassed, or on any account risked with the French, excepting in such operations as should be agreed upon, according to a general combination of all the forces that could be brought against them. The army of the Marquis of Romana was moved from Galicia to Ciudad Rodrigo; where it was placed under" the orders of the Duke del Parque.

A state of tranquillity now succeeded to the active operations of the preceding months; the French armies had been in almost constant movement since the entrance of Bonaparte into Spain, in the month of November. When he quitted the country to prepare for the German war, he had left his armies in possession of all the north of Spain; Soult afterwards added the north of Portugal. Victor was advanced to the confines of Andalusia, near Monasterio; and Sebastiani occupied La Mancha; Suchet was in force in Arragon, and St. Cyr was employed in the siege of the fortresses in Catalonia. The situation of these corps was now considerably changed. The north of Spain and Portugal was almost entirely free from the incursions of the French; the province of Estremadura was relieved from them; and a great portion of La Mancha was in the occupation of the Spanish armies. The French had therefore lost considerably during the last months; and, notwithstanding their activity and military talents, they had been forced to retire from the provinces which they had subdued, and to concentrate for their own defence, in a country which they believed, after the capture of Madrid, they had totally subjected. When Bonaparte re-crossed the Pyrenees, he directed his imperial eagles to be placed upon the towers of Lisbon; he proclaimed his empire in the Peninsula, and boasted that there no longer existed any force that was capable of obstructing the accomplishment of his imperial mandate. But the strength of patriotism in a whole people was as yet unknown to him. The constant reduction of his forces, the ever succeeding, evacuation of apparently conquered provinces by his troops, the never-ending conflicts in every corner of the Peninsula, have since convinced him that a great people with one intent and one resolution, with patriotism as their guide, are too powerful to be subdued, though they have neither armies nor military science to oppose to the invaders.

The British troops had been also in constant activity since the arrival of Lord Wellington in Portugal, they therefore required rest. It became then the interest of both French and English to preserve that state of tranquillity which had succeeded since the passage of the Tagus.

The state of Spain about this time, was most extraordinary; the whole people were hostile to the French, yet their exertions at the commencement of their struggle had so far surpassed any former efforts they had been called upon to make, that they now reposed in security, confiding their cause to the means which they had already provided, and sheltering themselves from any further calls, by the loud and re-echoed declarations that they were invincible. It was in vain to combat against this argument; if a doubt as to its validity was started, the instances of Moncey's retreat from Valencia and of Ney's from Galicia, were thought sufficient to remove all apprehensions, and to silence forever the discussion of the subject; the best informed amongst the Spaniards were carried away by feelings so congenial to their haughty spirits, and so well adapted to the indolence of their natures.

The defence of Saragossa and of Gerona convinced them that the attempt to conquer Spain would be unavailing, and they sunk at once into a security for which they since have most dearly paid. If at Granada, you questioned the public authorities as to the preparations they were making to bring new armies into the field, they answered by an account of what had already been produced. If in Valencia, the defeat which the French had already sustained there was a guarantee of the destruction which would await a second corps, that should attempt the invasion of their country; Murcia could boast the terror with which it had. inspired the enemy, since he had never ventured to attack it; and in this manner every part of Spain relied with confidence upon the levies which it had already produced, and looked upon its entire deliverance from a foreign yoke, as within little of being accomplished.

During the period of which we have been speaking, Marshal Ney commenced an operation against the corps of the Duke del Parque: that officer had collected his troops in a strong position at Tamanes; the French made a desperate assault upon him, but were repulsed with considerable loss. This action confirmed the Spaniards in the belief that they were invincible; and a general feeling was raised, that their armies should advance upon Madrid, and that the successes of Baylen would shrink before the glories that awaited them in the neighbourhood of the capital.

The disastrous termination of the German war seemed in no degree to shake the confidence of the Spanish nation; proud of its own feats, it disdained a feeling of dependency upon any other people for the success of its cause.

The government partook of the same sentiment; and, most singular to relate, during the period of this eventful repose from active operations, made not the slightest effort to prepare for the struggle which was to succeed.

The army of Lord Wellington which was cantoned upon the Guadiana became extremely sickly; and numbers of the officers and men fell victims to the disorders generated by the noxious exhalations of that river, and to the fatigues which, amidst the greatest privations, they had previously undergone. The Spaniards made no exertions to secure provisions for the army; so that it was incapable of active operations.

The Spanish government seized this opportunity to attempt a scheme, which will ever stand unrivalled in absurdity and folly. The Spanish army which was assembled at the Carolina formed an effective force of 48,000 men; it had been placed under the orders of General Eguia, when he marched with the greatest proportion of his army from Estremadura; but it had afterwards been entrusted to the command of General Arisaga, a very young and inexperienced officer; he was only a brigadier when he was appointed to this important station, but was advanced to the rank of a major-general upon assuming it.

It appears that this officer was befriended by a strong party of the ministers at Seville, who had considerable influence with the supreme government, although their views were hostile to it. He was appointed for the purpose of carrying their objects into effect; and every officer senior to him was removed, to enable him to assume the command. The other Spanish corps which communicated with the central one, were commanded by the Dukes of Albuquerque and Del Parque, both of superior rank to General Arisaga; it was, therefore, the object of his employers to prevent their cooperation with him, lest by taking upon themselves the direction of the forces, to which they were entitled by their rank, they should prevent the execution of the project the ministers had in view.

These persons conceived that it was possible to enter Madrid; and they are supposed to have purposed, in so doing, to effect a revolution, to displace the government of the Junta Suprema, and to seize it for themselves.

The capital was believed to be the most advantageous place for the execution of these projects; first, because the triumph of its successful deliverance would secure popularity to those who had effected it; and next, because the existing government had ever been most unpopular in that city. With these views, therefore, General Arisaga was ordered to break up at once from his position at La Carolina and to march directly upon Madrid. This order was neither communicated to Lord Wellington, nor to any of the Spanish generals in the command of other corps.

General Arisaga, in conformity with his instructions, moved with considerable rapidity through the whole of La Mancha, and arrived on the 8th of November upon the Tagus, in the neighbourhood of Ocaña. The French, who were surprised at the boldness of this operation, concentrated their troops behind the Tagus, and after a sharp *rencontre* with the Spanish advanced guard, upon the 12th, they passed that river and attacked the Spanish army. General Arisaga had placed his whole force in two columns of battalions, separated by a ravine, and with a corps in advance of considerable strength, which was in possession of a village which covered his front. The French began the engagement by the attack of this village; but, under cover of some ground about it, they turned the right column of the Spanish army, charged it, and in a very short time totally dispersed it. The left column was as yet untouched, but General Arisaga was so confounded by the destruction of his right, that he does not appear to have made any disposition for its retreat, or for the support of the attack that was coming upon it. The Spanish cavalry, which was retiring with considerable precipitation, first threw this corps into confusion by galloping through a considerable portion of it; the French, who were fast coming up with the remainder of it, completed its dispersion; and thus destroyed in a few hours the whole army that had been marched against them. The Spaniards lost their guns, their baggage, their equipments, and out of 45,000 stand of arms, not more than 13,000 were brought back to the Carolina. The loss in killed, wounded, and prisoners, was immense; a great portion of the soldiers, who had dispersed during the action, never returned to the army; so that the greatest number that was ever collected, of individuals who had been present at Ocaña, did not amount to more than 25,000 men.

So decisive a defeat produced great consternation throughout the country; the only considerable army that remained to fight for the cause of Spain had been totally destroyed; and to enlightened and unprejudiced minds, it was no longer doubtful that the French might at any time march, unresisted by any military force, to the walls of Cadiz. This opinion was far, however, from being general in Spain. All true Spaniards were yet bound to believe that the battle of Ocaña was unfortunate from some unforeseen accident; that such was never likely to happen again; and that the forces which were collected at the

Carolina would yet form an impenetrable barrier to the advance of the French armies and protect the Andalusias, till the necessary numbers should be collected to fall with certain destruction upon the forces of the invader. If a doubt was started upon any part of this position, one general answer was given, that a cat could not pass through the defile of Despeña Perros, much less a French army. Thus you were requested to be convinced, that no force the enemy could bring would ever succeed in penetrating to the southward of the Sierra Morena; or in subjugating the people of Andalusia.

Marshal Soult, who had been appointed major-general of the French armies a short time before the battle of Ocaña, seized the opportunity, which was offered by the destruction of the central army of Spain, to detach a considerable corps against the Duke del Parque, who had lately succeeded in occupying Salamanca. The French were fortunate enough to bring his army to action at Alba de Tormes, and, in spite of the good conduct of some of his troops, entirely to disperse it. The defeat of this corps laid the north of Portugal open to the incursions of the French; the whole of Castile fell into their possession; Salamanca became a depot, from whence they could prepare the means of a powerful attack and there no longer remained a force that could oppose or delay their operations.

Lord Wellington saw the absolute necessity of removing his army to the north of the Tagus to oppose the invasion which was thus preparing. He had no longer any Spanish armies that he could cooperate with; the only two of any considerable force with which he was in communication had brought destruction upon themselves, without either listening to his counsels, or communicating to him their movements; they were now no longer in a state to be of any assistance to him, nor could he protect them against the powerful reinforcements to the French which were arriving from Germany, and which bid fair to overrun the whole of the Peninsula.

Chapter 9
Andalusia

The system of war was now to be completely changed. When Lord Wellington entered Spain, the Spaniards had an army of considerable strength, with which he had hoped to cooperate with effect against a comparatively small and extended force of French. The tables were now reversed; the Spanish armies could scarcely be said to have any military existence; they had proved that while in strength they were not to be depended upon, much less were they to be looked to for any assistance in their present state.

The French were marching an army of more than 100,000 men into the country; so that a defensive war was the only one which could be carried on against them.

Lord Wellington was convinced that the hostility of the Spaniards to the French was not to be overcome: although their armies were beaten from the field, yet the determined opposition of the people repelled the yoke which was attempted to be forced upon them. The nature of the country was favourable to a protracted, desultory warfare; and its extent and poverty seemed to bid defiance to a subjection, which; to be made complete, would require a more considerable force than France seemed able to afford, or Spain could produce the means of supporting. As far as experience could lead to any conclusion as to the future, in the new warfare which the Spanish nation was waging against its invaders, there appeared no advantage to the enemy from the occupation of any part of the country, for any period of time. The moment a province was evacuated, it rose in more determined hostility, than it had shown before its invasion. No advantage accrued to the French from either violent or conciliating measures; they were always looked upon as enemies and, after months of peaceable occupation, if they exposed themselves unprotected by numbers in the provinces which they had considered as subdued, they were sure of meeting with the same hostility they had from the first experienced.

With this state of things to direct Lord Wellington in the system of warfare upon which he was called upon to decide, he felt no hesitation in prescribing to himself, and to the allies, a conduct which should protract the war; should lead the enemy to extend his forces; should encourage the whole people of the Peninsula to intercept his communications and should give the governments of the countries engaged in the contest, the opportunity of increasing and improving the more regular means of resistance or attack.

Lord Wellington moved his army in the beginning of December, from the neighbourhood of Badajos to the north of the Tagus. It arrived, in the first weeks of January, in the new cantonments which had been prepared for it, they extended from Coimbra to Pinhel, while a corps under Lieutenant General Hill was left at Abrantes. In this position the army went into winter-quarters: it was abundantly supplied, and was employed only in recruiting itself from the dreadful effects of the preceding campaign and the sickness which had followed it. Headquarters were placed at Viseu.

While Lord Wellington was employed in this movement, Marshal Soult concentrated the French armies in La Mancha; for the purpose of making an irruption into the southern provinces of Spain.

The British officers who had been at the Carolina were satisfied that, notwithstanding the boasted impossibility of forcing the Spanish army at the pass of Des Peña Perros, there was in reality nothing easier. The pass itself was strong, but no fortifications, which deserved that name, had been thrown up to defend it. The old road from Madrid, by the Puerto del Rey, was almost unobserved; and the force which was employed to defend the position of the Sierra Morena, which was fifty leagues in extent, did not exceed 25,000 men, most of them the unfortunate fugitives from the battle of Ocaña.

With such an army it would have been impossible for the most able commander to have defended the entry into Andalusia; but even that chance was denied the Spaniards, for they still had General Arisaga at their head. The Junta Suprema was urged to make some exertion to recruit the Spanish forces, and to prepare for the struggle which was fast approaching; but that body could only prove its patriotism by echoing the national cry, that Spaniards were invincible. Several nuns, who believed themselves inspired prophetesses, were produced to the loyal inhabitants of Seville to assure them that if ever the French should see the walls of that town, the fire of heaven would fall upon them, before they should reach its gates. In many other towns the same prophetic inspiration descended upon the nuns; they foretold in every instance the destruction which awaited the invaders, but the misfortunes they were themselves to suffer, appear not to have been so correctly foreseen by them.

The preparations of the French in La Mancha seemed, however, at last to have roused the Junta from its state of apathy; Seville and the world were called as witnesses of its new vigour, by a decree for the fabrication of 100,000 *knives*, to be distributed amongst the voluntary defenders of the country. This piece of absurdity will hardly be credited by those who were not at Seville at the moment; yet it is a fact which stands recorded amongst the vigorous measures of the Junta, and will hereafter be a standard to judge, of the hands to which the defence of Spain was at that time entrusted. The credit of the Junta, which had been fast declining, was completely destroyed by the promulgation of this decree; to raise itself again in the estimation of the public, it published an order for the assembling of the Cortes; but its race was nearly run, all confidence in it was gone, and a few days more completed the term of its existence.

Marshal Soult had terminated his preparations for the invasion of Andalusia, towards the end of December; he had collected a force of 50,000 men, and commenced his movements in two columns; the more considerable one, with the whole of his artillery, he destined to the attack of the principal pass by the Carolina; the other was directed to move by the mountain-road upon Cordova; neither of these corps experienced any resistance: the much-talked-of pass of Des Peña Perros was abandoned without a shot, and the Spanish army which was to defend it, retired toward Jaen. The corps which moved upon Cordova was equally successful. Marshal Soult directed a part of his army to pursue the Spaniards upon Jaen, which had been fortified at very great expense, but which surrendered a few hours after it was summoned. With the remainder of his army he moved with great rapidity upon Seville.

When the Junta Suprema was made acquainted with the successful eruption of the French, its first object was to escape to a place of safety, and it made choice of Cadiz for this object; but its members had considerable apprehensions, lest the populace, who were enraged against them, should impede their flight. They fell, however, upon a most extraordinary expedient to save themselves:—A bulletin was published by authority, and distributed throughout Seville, stating, that a courier to the British Minister had arrived, bringing dispatches from Lord Wellington, who was moving with the British army upon Salamanca, and was left with his advance within a few leagues of that place; that the courier had passed through the armies of the Dukes del Parque and Albuquerque, who were within a short distance of each other, and were about to fall upon the flank of Marshal Soult. Under cover of this communication, the whole of which was false, for no courier whatsoever had arrived at the British Minister's, nor were any of the movements making by any of the corps which were mentioned, the individuals who composed the junta, began to escape to Cadiz; the populace of Seville were not long, however, in discovering the imposition which had been practised upon them and a pursuit of the junta immediately commenced. Many of its members were seized upon the road to Cadiz, and imprisoned in the convent of the Cartjuo, near Xeres; they were afterwards carried to the Isla de Leon, where they were required to abdicate their authority, and appoint a regency. They concurred in these directions, and named General Castaños, who was but just released from the confinement in which they had placed him, the president of a board of regents, who were to govern the country in the name of Ferdinand the Seventh.

While these changes were effecting, the people of Seville reinstated the former junta of their province, and added the Marquis of Romana, the Duke of Albuquerque, and some English to its number; but this body had not time to act; Marshal Soult was already within a few days' march of the town: it constituted, however, the Marquis of Romana captain-general of Estremadura; and directed the Duke of Albuquerque, who had brought his corps with him from Estremadura, to take up a position at Carmona, to defend the approach to Seville. The army which the duke commanded was, however, too weak to resist the French; he therefore fell back upon their approach and, in spite of their efforts to prevent it, retired to the Isla de Leon. To this place Marshal Soult pursued him, and thus, in one movement, without a single action, reduced the whole of the southern provinces of Spain to the subjection of France. He extended his army to the walls of Gibraltar; he occupied Malaga, Granada, Jaen, Cordova, and Seville, and he prepared for the siege of Cadiz, which was the only bar to the complete reduction of Andalusia.

This operation was as rapid and as successful, as it was possible to execute. The great resources of the Spanish monarchy were reduced at one blow; the riches of Andalusia were abandoned to the enemy without a struggle; and the great nursery of the Spanish armies, the provinces from which innumerable bands of patriots might have been drawn, were at once delivered into the hands of the invader. Some persons thought, that, in the tame relinquishment of these treasures, they perceived a readiness in the Spaniards to abandon the cause for which they had, till that moment, so gloriously been struggling; but the fallacy of that opinion has since been proved. The revolution in Spain had found that country merged in all the vices of its former weak and imbecile governments. Spain had not for many years been called into any extensive warfare; it was without any military organization; it was unused to great exertions; yet the people were proud of their former exploits and, without adverting to the changes which had taken place, believed themselves and their armies as invincible, as they had been during the most brilliant periods of their history. The nation had been long sunk in ignorance and oppression; it had no military science, no commanders to whom it could look for assistance, no army that could defend it; yet it had universally risked a contest with the greatest military power the world had ever seen and which had armies, more powerful than any the nation could oppose to them, within its territory. Elated by the first successes at Baylen and Saragossa, the Spaniards afterwards sunk into their former habits of indolence. Pride dictated to them a feeling of security, which reason would have made them doubt; but their succeeding reverses never changed their first opinions, although the total want of confidence, in their generals or their governments, made them little anxious to place themselves under their directions. The Supreme Junta, which had been established to rule the country in circumstances of the greatest difficulty, was totally unable to call forth the energies of the nation. The same intrigues, which had existed under the long reign of the Prince of the Peace, continued under its auspices. The want of money was soon felt throughout the country, the Junta was unacquainted with the means of obtaining it, and was not very scrupulous in the application of the sums it received. The army was unpaid, and was consequently without discipline. The generals were unsupported by the government, which was too weak to uphold them in the execution of their duty. The Juntas of the different provinces yielded but a limited obedience to the central one; they were composed of persons who looked most to their own advantage in the high situations to which they had been called, and who were unwilling to make exertions, the burthen of which would fall upon themselves. In this state of things, the declaration that Spain was invincible, was the readiest mode of abstaining from those efforts which were necessary to make her so, but which accorded too little with the character of the people who were to make them. Andalusia was in consequence totally unprepared for the blow which was struck at her. Her population however was not the less hostile to the invaders; there was no point round which it could rally in the hour of danger, the people sunk under the power of their enemies, but they still were Spaniards; they moaned the cruel fate which had attended them, but they remained steadfast through all their misery to the great cause of their nation and their independence.

CHAPTER 10

The Coa & Almeida

While Marshal Soult was employed in overrunning the southern provinces of Spain, General Suchet, who in the month of June had defeated the army of General Blake on the heights of Santa Maria, marched with a considerable corps to reduce the kingdom of Valencia. He reached, with little opposition, the walls of that capital; but the resistance of the people was there so determined, and the means he brought with him so inadequate to the task imposed upon him, that he retired from the country without having effected any object for which he had commenced his operation. He resumed his position in Arragon, and afterwards employed himself in the siege of the fortresses of Catalonia.

The first act of the new regency of Spain was to request Lord Wellington to afford some assistance from his army, for the garrison and defence of Cadiz. Lord Wellington, in compliance, detached to that place a force of 3,000 men, which arrived there after a short passage from Lisbon, and which contributed materially to its defence. The siege was begun under the directions of Marshal Soult, in the end of January, 1810; and it lasted almost without interruption till August 1812.

The great body of reinforcements that about this time arrived to the French armies in Spain took the direction of Salamanca: it became therefore evident that an attack on Portugal was determined upon. Marshal Ney placed the advance of his corps upon the Agueda, and threatened to invest Ciudad Rodrigo; but the difficulty of obtaining provisions in the winter season prevented him from undertaking that operation till later in the year. A detachment from the French army attacked a part of the British rifle corps, under Colonel Beckwith, at Barba del Puerco, but was repulsed with considerable loss. This was the first affair which took place between the army, which was entitled that of Portugal, and the British corps destined to defend that kingdom; it was a sample of what its whole body was afterwards to meet with. Marshal Ney, commanded in chief at Salamanca; General Junot was second to him. These officers were anxious to engage Lord Wellington to break up from his winter quarters, and, if possible, to draw him into the open country of Castile. With this view General Junot was detached to Astorga, to undertake the siege of that town. Lord Wellington was not induced to depart from the system which he had prescribed to himself, by the movements of the enemy; he felt, that however important the possession of Astorga might be to the cause he was employed in defending, yet it was more essential to maintain his army in the positions it occupied; and to preserve it unbroken for the great contest which, he foresaw, it would soon be called upon to maintain.

He remained, therefore, in perfect quiet, recruiting his army, and giving the Portuguese the opportunity of forming and improving their troops. Astorga was taken after a defence of five weeks, and Junot returned with his corps to the neighbourhood of Salamanca. Marshal Soult detached General Regnier with his corps to operate in Estremadura against the Spanish troops, of which the Marquis of Romana had the command. Lieutenant General Hill, who had been left at Abrantes with a corps of 13,000 men, British and Portuguese, advanced to Portalegre, to cooperate with them, and to prevent the investment of Elvas or Badajos. He was directed, however, not to engage in offensive operations. General Regnier effected little. He had several engagements with parts of the Marquis of Romana's corps, but none of them were productive of any decisive results.

In the beginning of May, Lord Wellington was apprized of

some movements in the French army, which indicated an advance, in strength, upon Ciudad Rodrigo; he lost not a moment in putting his army in motion, and placing it on the frontiers of Portugal. He established his headquarters at Celorico, and his divisions at Pinhel, Alverca, Guarda, Trancoso, and along the valley of the Mondego, as far as Cea, and upon the opposite bank of that river at Fornos, Mangualde, and Viseu. He determined in this position to await the movements of the enemy; he could decide from it, in security, either to cooperate in the defence of Ciudad Rodrigo, or to attack the French army if an opportunity was given him. Marshal Ney moved, however, but a small corps to the neighbourhood of Ciudad Rodrigo; the roads from Salamanca were still extremely bad, and impracticable for a train of artillery; he gave up therefore any further object. Marshal Massena was at this time sent by Bonaparte to take the command of the army of Portugal, and he arrived at Salamanca in the end of May. The corps of General Regnier was added to his army, which was now composed of the 6th corps under Ney, the 8th corps under Junot and the second corps under Regnier. Massena brought this latter corps from the south-of the Tagus to the neighbourhood of Coria, from which place it was in communication with him; and Lieutenant General Hill, who had been directed to observe it, made a corresponding movement, crossed the Tagus at Villa Velha, and established his headquarters at Sarzedas. Marshal Mortier was detached by Soult to supply the place of Regnier in Estremadura; and the Marquis of Romana remained in observation of the corps which that officer had brought with him. A reinforcement of some regiments which had returned from the Walcheren expedition was sent about this time, under Major General Leith, from England. As the men were extremely sickly, Lord Wellington did not choose to bring them to the army; they were embodied with some regiments of Portuguese; and placed upon the Zezere, where General Leith commanded the whole corps. The force of the allied army destined for the defence of Portugal, may be computed at the following amount:

The Corps with Lord Wellington	30,000
The Corps with Lieutenant General Hill	14,000
The Corps with Major General Leith	<u>10,000</u>
	54,000
In cooperation with this force was	
A corps of Portuguese Militia	10,000
The corps under the Marquis Romana	<u>12,000</u>
	22,000
Making a total of	76,000
The French force under Massena was:	
The Infantry of the 2nd, 6th and 8th corps	62,000
The Cavalry	6,000
The Artillery	<u>4,000</u>
Total	72,000
To this were afterwards joined two Divisions of the 9th corps under Count Erlon	10,000
The remaining division of this corps under General Claparede	8,000
The corps of Marshal Mortier which cooperated to the south of the Tagus	13,000
Making a total of	103,000

These numbers are the very lowest at which the French army can be calculated. Bonaparte always called the force under Massena alone 100,000 men; and the French officers, before the invasion of Portugal, gave the same account of the numbers with which they were to overwhelm us.

In comparing the amount of the two armies, the description of force of which they were composed should be taken into consideration. The Portuguese had as yet been perfectly untried; and their militia was so defective in organization as to be evidently unfit for the operations of a campaign.

Yet Lord Wellington was not alarmed at the disparity of numbers, or the superior organization of the troops of the enemy; he relied upon his own genius to baffle their efforts, and combined his plans with reference to the troops he had to command.

In the latter part of the year 1809, while Lord Wellington was still at Badajos, he had contemplated the possibility of his being attacked in Portugal by a superior force; he had considered the nature of the country he should have to defend, as well as the system of warfare which would most tend to support the contest in the Peninsula: he looked upon the preservation of his own army as the guarantee of the future triumph of the cause he was to maintain. The extension of the enemy, in the occupation of distant provinces, must be a source of weakness to him; the lengthening his communications must add considerably to his embarrassments. Lord Wellington, therefore, fixed upon the heights of Sobral and Torres Vedras, as the best positions in which he could collect his army, and offer battle to the superior forces of his enemy.

With such a determination, he spared no pains in fortifying and strengthening these places; the range of positions connected with, them extended from the Tagus at Alhandra, to the sea at the mouth of the Zizandra; the accessible points were occupied with forts; and every resource was employed to make a line of defence, in which so eventful a contest was to be decided, as formidable as art, combined with its natural advantages, could render it. The early decision of Lord Wellington was supported by the events which succeeded each other in the early parts of the year 1810. The great force of the enemy which menaced Portugal, and the total destruction of all the effective Spanish armies which could cooperate with the British in defence of it, confirmed Lord Wellington in the wisdom of his plan of retreat.

The French had a force in Spain of not less than 300,000 men; this army was distributed over almost every part of the country; Galicia, Valencia, and Murcia, were the only provinces that were free, the rest were in the occupation of the enemy. The amount of this force, when collected, was sufficient to overwhelm the small numbers of the allies that were in a state of military organization in the Peninsula; but from great extension, it became unequal to the task imposed upon it. It was employed in completing the subjugation of the provinces that had been conquered; and yet that object was not advancing, although the force was frittered away in seeking to accomplish it. The animosity of the people was working in silence the destruction of the French armies. Every succeeding day brought reports of skirmishes, or individual *rencontre*s, in which the enemy were worsted, and no account represented any part of Spain as diminishing in its hostility, or as being treated with more confidence, or relied upon with greater security, by the French.

The army of Marshal Massena, while attempting the conquest of Portugal, could lend no aid towards the reduction of the people in the Peninsula. As long as it was in observation of the British troops, whether on the Spanish frontier or in the lines of Lisbon, it could as little assist the views of Bonaparte in reducing the country to obedience; the destruction of Lord Wellington's army could alone enable Massena to fulfil the objects of his imperial master.

The preventing that catastrophe formed the basis of Lord Wellington's plans for the campaign. He was neither strong enough, nor had he any wish, to undertake offensive operations: the state of Spain was not such as to make them advisable; they must necessarily be commenced at considerable risk against a superior army; and if they were unsuccessful the cause of the Peninsula was lost. By the plan which Lord Wellington had determined, upon, he promised to preserve his army, to increase its discipline, to augment its numbers, to draw the French into a country where their means of subsistence would be confined, and where their force would not be sufficient to maintain even their communications with the depots, which must necessarily be placed at a distance from them.

Massena advanced from Salamanca in the beginning of June, to commence the siege of Ciudad Rodrigo; he brought with him a considerable train of artillery, and expected the place would surrender upon being summoned. But it was defended with considerable ability and valour, and was only yielded into the hands of the enemy upon the 18th of July, after the breaches were practicable and the principal defences destroyed. Many persons at the time conceived that Lord Wellington had seen the fall of this fortress with considerable indifference, since he had made no movement to relieve it; but it is only necessary to point out the results of victory or defeat to the different armies, to show the propriety of Lord Wellington's determination not to risk a general action. To attack the French he must have crossed the Coa and the Agueda; if he had been defeated, he would have had great difficulty in repassing those rivers, and saving the wrecks of his army. He would no longer have been able to provide for the defence of Portugal with a beaten army; he must have evacuated the country. If he beat the French they would have retired upon reinforcements, and would have been prepared to advance upon him again in a very short time. Lord Wellington would have had to lament the brave men he must have lost in an action, which would but have relieved Ciudad Rodrigo for a short time, as he must afterwards have abandoned it to the superior numbers of the enemy. His army must also have been considerably weakened; and most likely would have been unequal to the task afterwards to be imposed upon it, in the defence of Portugal.

Soon after the fall of Ciudad Rodrigo, the British advanced guard, under Major General Crawford, retired from the fort of La Conception, and was placed in a position under the walls of Almeida. Lord Wellington directed this corps to fall back across the Coa but, from some misapprehension, these orders were not executed, and it was attacked upon the 24th of July. The French had the whole corps of Ney engaged in this affair; it manoeuvred under cover of its cavalry upon the right of Major General Crawford, who did not decide upon his retreat until it had gained his flank. The British and Portuguese troops behaved with great gallantry, but they could not cope with numbers so superior to their own; they retired across the bridge over the Coa in some confusion, but formed to defend it, and repulsed the repeated attacks of the enemy to gain possession of it. Major General Crawford had been previously, for a considerable time, with his advanced guard close to the French army. During the siege of Ciudad Rodrigo, he had maintained a communication with the place, and had assisted Don Julian Sanches in his successful effort to leave it. This officer, who had for a long time commanded a corps of guerrillas, and who had been most fortunate in his enterprises against the enemy, was enclosed within the walls of this fortress, by the rapidity with which the French had invested it. Massena was aware of the circumstance, and vowed vengeance against this chief of *banditti*, as he was pleased to designate him. But Don Julian determined to force his way through the besieging army. He formed his corps in close column, placed his wife by his side at the head of it, and left the town soon after dark. As soon as he was challenged by the French sentries, he moved at full gallop upon them; cut down those that he met with, and continued his course till he had passed through the army. He arrived in safety at the quarters of Major General Crawford, and soon after retaliated upon several of the enemy the vengeance they had threatened to inflict upon him.

On the day on which Ciudad Rodrigo surrendered, General Crawford, while making a reconnaissance, fell in with a strong patrol from the French army; he engaged in an affair with it, which did not turn out successfully; the French infantry repulsed three successive charges of the British cavalry, in one of which Colonel Talbot, of the 14th Light Dragoons, was killed, and profiting by a mistake amongst our own troops, who took each other for enemies, it retired with little loss to the corps which was supporting it. The cavalry which accompanied it was taken.

Marshal Massena invested Almeida on the 24th of July, immediately after the affair under the walls of that place with the corps of Major General Crawford. Lord Wellington retired from Alverca, where he had placed his headquarters during the siege of Ciudad Rodrigo, to his former station at Celorico; he also drew back the divisions that were at Pinhel and Trancoso, and

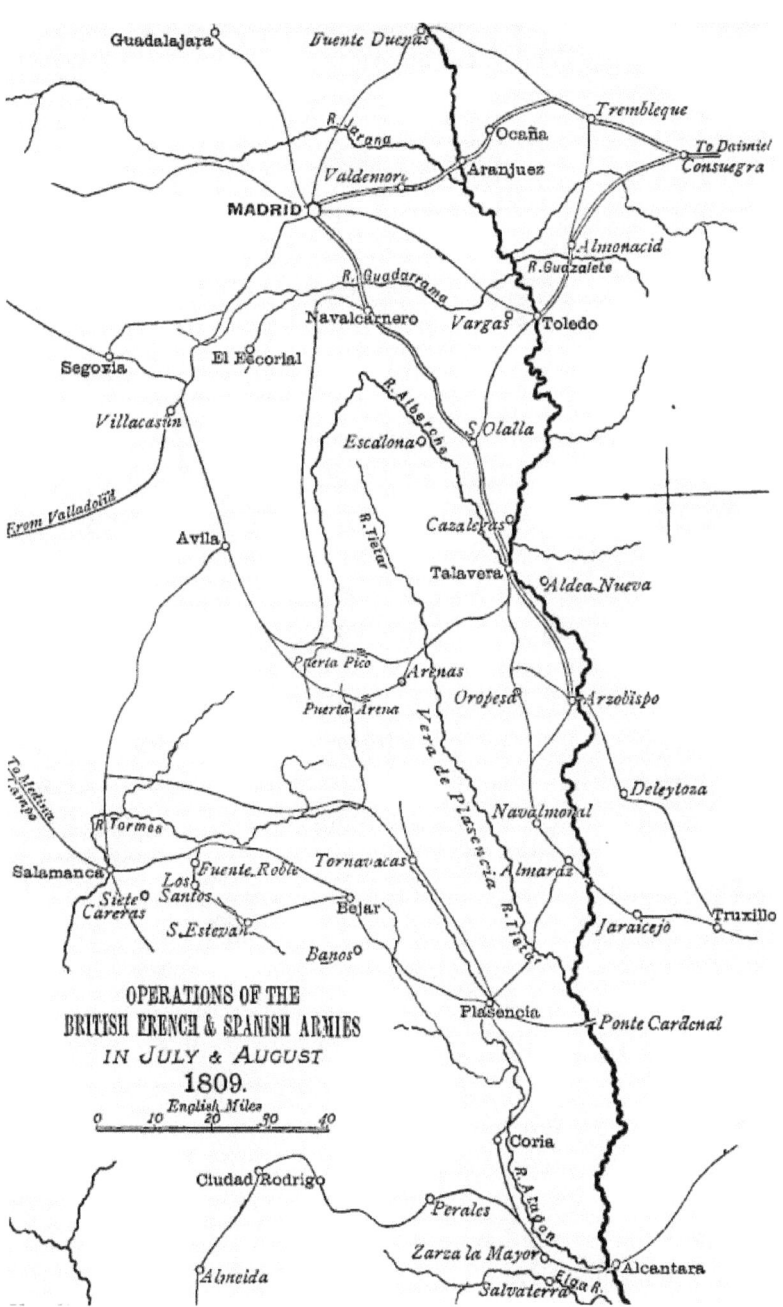

placed them in rear of Celorico, along the valley of the Mondego. He was thus prepared to commence his retreat upon the lines, in case the enemy had determined to push forward, before the capture of Almeida. Massena preferred, however, the surer game, and commenced the siege of that place.

He was considerably delayed in his operations by the nature of the ground, and was not able to open his fire upon it till the 23rd of August. Lord, Wellington determined to assist the place in its defence, although he did not choose to risk an action to relieve it; he moved up his whole army as soon as the firing had commenced from the trenches, and, on the 27th of August, had determined to place it upon the banks of the Coa. In the course of that day, however, Lord Wellington, while reconnoitring, was surprised to find that all firing had ceased about Almeida. The telegraph, by which he communicated with it, no longer sent him any information, and he was afraid it had surrendered; he observed a person walking upon the glacis, which confirmed his suspicions, and he was informed of a considerable explosion which had taken place the night preceding. Lord Wellington immediately ordered his army to be ready to fall back to its positions in the rear, but the place recommenced its firing about ten o'clock at night; it ceased, however, at twelve; and the following morning, in a skirmish with the enemy's cavalry, a German sergeant, in the French service, called to a dragoon of the 1st German hussars, and told him to apprize his General that Almeida had surrendered. The order for the retreat was soon after given; and the allied army was again placed in its position, in the valley of the Mondego.

The loss of Almeida, after only three days firing, was a severe mortification to Lord Wellington; he found afterwards, that an order which he had given when he visited the place in the February preceding, to remove the great magazine from the centre of the town to one of the casemates, had not been executed; that a shell having fallen near the door of this depot, while some men were employed in getting powder, the whole provision of that article for the garrison had been blown up;

the town had been nearly destroyed by the explosion; the ramparts had been materially injured; and the place had been left without the means of defence. In this situation the governor, General Cox, endeavoured to capitulate, upon being allowed to retire with his garrison; but the Portuguese officer, who was sent to negotiate, and who is the only instance of a traitor among the officers of that nation who have acted with the British army, betrayed the disastrous situation of the place, and refused to return within it. Marshal Massena insisted upon unconditional surrender, which Brigadier General Cox refused; the firing recommenced, as has been already stated, but at midnight the town was surrendered.

The Marquis de Alorna, who was with the French army, desired the Portuguese garrison to enter the service of France, and to become a part of a Portuguese legion, of which he was to be the commander; but the whole of the men and officers refused. They were then threatened with every sort of persecution; they were menaced with the utmost rigour of the law as traitors to their country; but if they would enlist under the French banners, they were promised protection and advantage. Seeing no other mode of escaping from a treatment so contrary to every principle of justice, the garrison consented to serve under the Marquis de Alorna; but its object was the reverse of what the French expected; the moment the individuals were restored to liberty, they planned the means of returning to their army and, on the third day from the time of their enlistment, there remained with the French out of the whole 20th Regiment, a squadron of cavalry and a company of artillery, but thirty men and a few officers, who had been detected at the moment they also were escaping. These troops were immediately re-formed, upon their return to Portugal and the 20th Regiment particularly distinguished itself throughout the campaign that followed.

An incident which took place on the night of the surrender of Almeida, deserves to be mentioned, to show the hostility of the Portuguese peasantry to the French. Colonel Pavetti, the chief of the *gens d'armerie* of France, in Spain, had gone to Almeida with Marshal Massena, when he left his headquarters at the fort of La Conception, to induce the garrison to surrender; when the firing recommenced, Colonel Pavetti, who was unwell, set out upon his return to his quarters; he was accompanied by a lieutenant-colonel, a captain, and twelve men. The night was extremely dark and stormy, and he lost his way. He met with a Portuguese shepherd, whom he took for his guide, and who promised to conduct him (the vengeance of these Frenchmen hanging over him) to the fort of La Conception. But this peasant could not resist his feelings of animosity; he found courage to mislead the party and under the pretence of having missed his way, brought it to his own village. He persuaded Colonel Pavetti to put up for the night in the house of the Jues de Fora, and pretended that he would procure provisions for him. Instead, however, of employing himself in that way, he collected the inhabitants, fell upon the French, killed them all, except the colonel, whom he beat most severely, and his servant who stated himself to be a German. The next day the colonel was brought, with two ribs broken and other damages, to the headquarters of Lord Wellington, where he was attended to, and afterwards sent prisoner to England.

To appreciate this event, it must be remembered that it took place in the middle of an army of 60,000 Frenchmen; that their revenge awaited those who were concerned in it; but that, notwithstanding, the animosity of the Portuguese was too strong to be resisted by any calculations of the retaliation which was likely to follow the act that was committed.

It will not be uninteresting to cite a trait of the character of Colonel Pavetti. Lord Wellington treated him with great kindness; bought the horse which had belonged to him of the peasants, returned it to him, and asked him to his table. While at dinner, this officer took an opportunity of stating to Lord Wellington that the Duchess of Abrantes was with her husband Junot; he added, *"Qu'elle était grosse, et qu'elle comptoit faire ses couches dans son duche."*[3]

---

3. Abrantes was at that time 150 miles behind our army, and throughout the whole succeeding campaigns, it was never taken by the enemy.

Lord Wellington took little notice of this impertinence; but General Alava, a Spanish officer, who was attached to the British headquarters, answered, *"Qu'il ferait bien de faire savoir à madame la duchesse, qu'elle eut garde de ces messieurs habillés en rouge, car ils étaient de très mauvais accoucheurs."*

During the sieges of Ciudad Rodrigo and Almeida, General Regnier had continually made movements with his corps upon Castel Branco, Pena-Macor, &c., with a view of inducing Lieutenant General Hill to leave the positions he occupied and to expose himself to an attack, which was meditated upon him from a part of the force under Massena, as well as from Regnier. It was also hoped that Lord Wellington might be induced to venture an attack upon Regnier's corps, which seemed exposed, but which Massena was prepared to support with his whole army.

Lord Wellington, however, was faithful to the system he had prescribed to himself; no artifice could draw him from the position which made his retreat secure; and Massena was at last obliged to come into Portugal, to seek him upon the ground he had chosen for his operations. Detachments of French were also sent upon Lord Wellington's left, with the same view of engaging him to break up from the positions he occupied; but all these movements failed in their object.

From the neighbourhood of Almeida there are three roads which lead directly to the centre of Portugal; that on the right by Trancoso to Viseu, the centre by Celorico to Fornos Mangualde and Viseu; the third by Celorico, Villa Cortes, Pinhancos, Puente de Marcella, and from hence to Coimbra and Thomar; from Viseu the road also leads by Busaco to Coimbra. The right and centre roads were extremely bad; so much so, that Lord Wellington condemned a considerable part of them as improper for artillery; he chose the road to Puente de Marcella as the fittest for his operations, and bestowed the greatest pains in improving it.

After the fall of Almeida, he had placed the infantry of his own corps along this road with the rear divisions, as far back as Puente de Marcella. The corps of Major General Leith was moved from the Zezere to Thomar, so as to be within reach for any assistance that might be required from it; and Lieutenant General Hill was kept at Sarzedas to cover the road along the Tagus upon Abrantes and Lisbon; but was directed to be prepared to move by the road of Formosa and Pedragoa Grande, to Puente de Marcella, in case Lord Wellington should require him to do so. The cavalry was in front of the whole army, and had its advanced posts at Alverca.

CHAPTER 11
Busaco

Massena commenced his march into Portugal upon the 16th of September; his army advanced in three corps; the 8th corps under Junot, moved by Pinhel upon Trancoso, the 6th corps under Ney, upon Alverca; and the 2nd corps, under Regnier, upon Guarda; the British cavalry retired to Celorico. The next day the two latter corps moved into Celorico; from which place they were observed to take the road to Fornos. As soon as Lord Wellington was persuaded that the enemy had made choice of that road, and that no part of their army was moving upon the road by the Tagus, he sent directions to Lieutenant General Hill to break up from Sarzedas, and to move by Pedragoa Grande, to the Puente de Marcella; he moved the corps of Major General Leith to the same place from Thomar, and he withdrew his own divisions with the view of collecting the whole army upon the Sierra of Busaco.

Marshal Massena had commenced his operations with the hopes of turning the left of Lord Wellington, and of reaching Coimbra before the British army could be collected to oppose him; he had been induced to believe that Lord Wellington had prepared to meet him at the Puente de Marcella; but he hoped that by this movement on the right of the Mondego, he should turn that position, and find Lord Wellington unprepared to assemble in any other. He was miserably deceived. Lord Wellington was aware of the nature of the roads the enemy had fixed upon for his movements; he calculated the delays he would meet with, and arranged his plans accordingly. He directed a portion of the militia that was at Lamego under the orders of Colonel Trant to march upon Sardao; the rest was directed to move upon Trancoso and Celorico, upon the rear of the enemy, to intercept their communication with Almeida.

Marshal Massena arrived at Viseu upon the 19th of September; his artillery had suffered so much from the badness of the roads that he was obliged to remain there for some days to repair it. General Junot joined him at this place from Trancoso, so that the whole French army was collected there. On the 23rd the advanced patrols of the British and French armies met each other near St. Comba de Dao. The bridge over the Cris, by which the great road to Coimbra passes, was blown up; but the following day the French advanced guard passed that river, and the greatest part of the British retired to the heights of Busaco, where the whole army was collecting. On the 25th Marshal Massena joined his advanced guard, and on the 26th pushed forward to the foot of the position which was occupied by Lord Wellington.

The ridge of heights upon which the British army was posted runs nearly north and south, from a point about four miles to the north of Busaco, to the confluence of the river Alva and the Mondego; the extreme points are nearly fifteen miles distant. Two great roads to Coimbra cross over this Sierra, the one close to the convent of Busaco, the other four miles to the southward of it, at St. Antonio de Cantaro. The corps of Lieutenant General Hill, which had made a most rapid though difficult march from Sarzedas, arrived upon the Mondego on the evening of the 26th, and was directed to move into the right of the position of Busaco early on the following morning. Lord Wellington had made a road along the heights, by which his flanks communicated, and in this situation he awaited the attack of the enemy.

We may be allowed for a moment to consider the brilliancy of the movement by which the allied army had thus been collected. Massena conceived that he should surprise his antagonist by the rapidity of his march upon his flank; the British officers generally thought that it would be impossible to oppose him before he had possessed himself of Coimbra; and the corps of Lieutenant General Hill was universally thought to be totally beyond the reach of the army of Lord Wellington. Marshal Massena for a long time disbelieved the fact of its junction at Busaco; and after he had been convinced of it, denied the possibility of its having marched from Sarzedas. Yet Lord Wellington, in spite of the difficulties opposed to him, of the able movements intended to surprise him, and of the triumphant predictions of his adversary, collected his force from situations in which it seemed totally divided from him, and was prepared to fight the enemy with the whole strength of the allied army, without having lost a single man in the attainment of his object. The corps of militia under Colonel Trant, which had been ordered to Sardao, from whence it was to have moved into the Sierra of Caramula, was the only one which had not reached the ground assigned to it; this failure was occasioned by some false information as to the possession of a pass by the enemy, which obliged that corps to move by a circuitous road through Oporto. It arrived upon the Vouga on the 28th, but too late to effect the object for which it was intended.

On the morning of the 27th of September the whole French army was arrayed in front of the British position, from whence every part of it was distinctly to be seen. The corps of Marshal Ney was formed in close columns at the foot of the bill opposite the convent of Busaco. The corps of General Regnier was opposite the third division of British under Major General Picton, and prepared to advance by the road to Coimbra, which passed over the height by St. Antonio de Cantaro. The corps of General Junot was in reserve with the greater part of the cavalry, and was posted upon some rising ground about a league in the rear of Marshal Ney.

The battle commenced by a fire from the light troops of both armies, in advance of the position which was occupied by the allies; a detachment from the corps of Marshal Ney next made an attack upon a village in front of the light division, which was ceded with little opposition. This village, although of im-

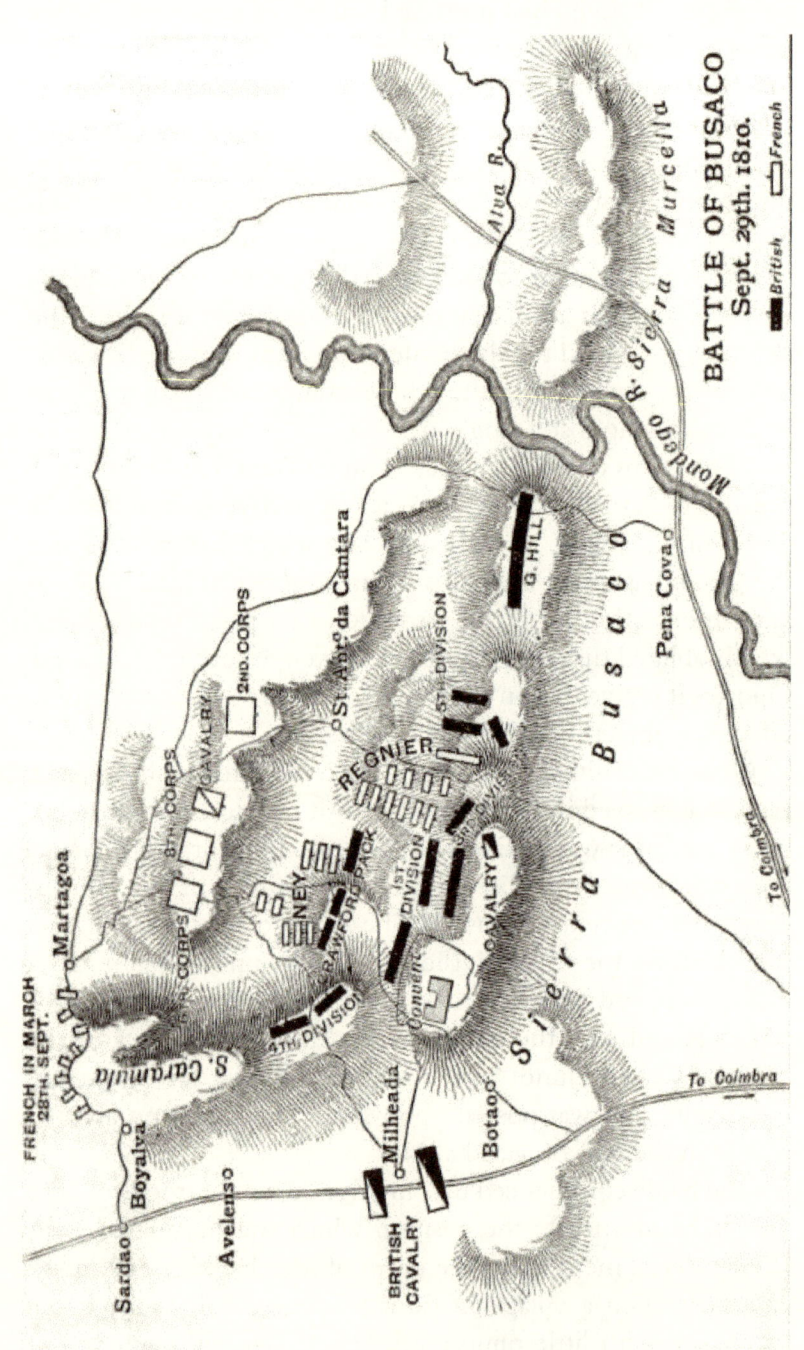

portance to the allied army, was without the position in which Lord Wellington had determined to receive the enemy's attack; he therefore abandoned it, choosing rather to suffer some annoyance from its possession by the enemy, than risk the chance of an action to maintain it in less advantageous ground than the position he had fixed upon.

Marshal Massena was now convinced that he must fight Lord Wellington upon his own ground; he therefore directed General Regnier to advance to the assault of the position in his front, while the 1st division of Marshal Ney's corps, supported by the other two, and a great proportion of artillery, was ordered to establish itself upon the heights occupied by the light division. General Regnier first brought his corps into action; the British regiments opposed to him had not reached the positions that were assigned to them; and, for a moment, a considerable column of French possessed itself of a point within our line. Major General Picton instantly marched against this column with a few companies which he had collected; Major General Lightburne's brigade, directed by Lord Wellington, moved upon its right, while the 88th, 45th, and Colonel Douglass's regiment of Portuguese, attempted to gain its left; the troops with Major General Picton, however, first dislodged the enemy by a most brilliant attack with the bayonet, driving him, though infinitely superior in numbers, from the strong ground he had got possession of; the other regiments came up in time to harass him in his retreat; and the arrival of Major General Leith's division, which took place at this moment, convinced General Regnier that he had better discontinue a contest, in which he had so little prospect of success. He withdrew his divisions, therefore, and formed upon the ground from which he had originally moved.

During this attack, Marshal Ney formed a part of his corps in column of mass, and directed it to ascend the height upon the right of the village, of which he had before obtained possession. The ground was extremely steep, and the column was but little annoyed in its ascent; as soon, however, as it had gained the summit, the guns attached to the light division opened a most destructive fire upon it, and the division charged it with the bayonet. The column was overthrown in an instant; the riflemen charged its flanks while Major General Crawford pursued it down the hill; the foremost regiments of the column were almost totally destroyed, General Simon wounded and taken, and the whole division completely routed.

The expression of a French soldier engaged in this attack, who was afterwards taken, *"Qu'il se laissa rouler du haut en bas de la montagne, sans savoir comment il échappa,"* best explains the mode in which the remnants of this column escaped. The allies pursued it across the valley, and thus put an end to the sanguine expectations of the, enemy, and to their boasted promise, of driving us like sheep from our position.

The rest of the day was occupied by an incessant fire between the light troops of the two armies; Marshal Massena had placed a considerable number of battalions in the road, which extended along the ravine, at the foot of the ridge on which we were formed; and he had hoped to induce Lord Wellington to reinforce the troops that were engaged with these battalions, and by that means to get him into an action of some consequence, out of the position which he occupied. This system had frequently been successful to the French; the commanders who have been opposed to them have been unwilling to allow their too near approach to their army, and have continued to reinforce the advanced posts, till the greater part of their troops had been drawn into an action, away from the ground on which they had decided to accept a battle; but Lord Wellington was not thus to be imposed upon; he directed the light troops, when pressed, to retire, and to give the enemy an opportunity of attacking his position, if he could persuade himself to do so.

At the approach of night, Marshal Massena having lost all hopes of succeeding against the allies, withdrew his troops from the advanced positions he occupied, and placed them at some distance in the rear, near the ground which was occupied by General Junot. Major General Crawford then sent to the officer who commanded in the village, which had been ceded in the morning, telling him that the possession of it was necessary to his corps, and therefore directing him to abandon it. The officer refused, with a declaration that he would die in defence of the post he was entrusted with. Major General Crawford immediately ordered six guns to open upon him, and some companies of the 43rd and Rifle Corps to charge the village. The French were instantly driven out of it, and the advanced post of the light division put in possession of it.

The battle of Busaco was thus terminated. The French lost 10,000 men killed, wounded, and prisoners, in the course of the day; and Marshal Massena was first enabled to form an estimate of the talents of the general, and the bravery of the troops which he was directed to drive headlong into the sea.

On the morning of the 28th, the two armies maintained their respective positions; towards the middle of the day, however, the French were observed to be retiring; they set fire to the woods to conceal their movement, but the height of Busaco so commanded the whole country, that their march wais distinctly seen.

Lord Wellington had been extremely anxious for the arrival of the corps of militia, under Colonel Trant, upon the Sierra of Caramula, the road over which communicated from Viseu to the great road from Oporto to Coimbra, near Sardao, Bamfiela and Avelans. This was the only pass by which the positions of the Sierra of Busaco could be turned, and there were parts of it so extremely difficult, that if this corps of militia had had the necessary time to destroy the bridges, and to avail itself of the positions afforded by the ravines which intersect the road, it might have opposed a most decisive resistance to the advance of the enemy. Lord Wellington did not choose to detach any part of the force which he considered as his effective army, to execute his object in this Sierra; such a corps might be cut off from him, or might have great difficulty in rejoining him; and he was resolved never to depart from his determination, that the great contest for the possession of Portugal should be fought by his whole army, and in a position which should leave the event as little doubtful as was possible in military operations.

The corps of Colonel Trant did not form a part of the force which Lord Wellington had decided to keep with him; he intended it for the defence of Oporto, to which place its retreat was not likely to be interrupted from the Sierra of Caramula; it had therefore been ordered to occupy the latter position; but Lord Wellington would not supply its absence by any other detachment.

As soon as Lord Wellington perceived the retreat of the enemy, he suspected that his object was to pass by the road just described. Colonel Trant had arrived upon the Vouga, late on the 28th; Lord Wellington was already aware, that a considerable corps of the enemy was by that time in possession of the Sierra, he therefore gave up the hope of seeing it occupied and in the same night withdrew his whole army from Busaco, moving with his own corps into Coimbra; and directing Lieut.-General Hill to move by Thomar to Santarem. The cavalry was placed in observation of the enemy, and was directed to cover Lord Wellington's movement to the rear.

Colonel Trant was ordered to post his corps along the north bank of the Vouga; and a part of the militia from Lamego was ordered to enter Viseu in the enemy's rear.

CHAPTER 12

The Lines at Torres Vedras

The situation of the French army began at this time to wear a less promising appearance; its communication with Spain was totally cut off; its supply of provisions was nearly exhausted; it had no means of obtaining subsistence but from the country; and the total evacuation of it by the inhabitants, of which, according to the French accounts, they had not seen twenty since their entry into Portugal, made this last resource extremely precarious. The allies, on the contrary, had beat the whole French army; they had gained confidence in themselves; the Portuguese troops had behaved with great bravery; the army relied with implicit faith on its commander; and it felt that, notwithstanding his movement to the rear, he was not afraid of encountering the enemy, but was leading it to stronger positions than the one in which he had already beaten him.

Marshal Massena appears at this time to have felt the difficulty of his situation. He had two lines of conduct open to him, either to rest satisfied with the progress he had made, and to endeavour to re-establish his communications with Spain, or to push forward in pursuit of the allies. The first would have been extremely difficult, he would have weakened his army by detaching to his rear, he would have suffered considerably from want of provisions till the supplies should have reached him and he would have exposed himself to an attack from Lord Wellington, while reduced in numbers. He was, besides, assured that there were no positions which the allies could take up in the vicinity of Lisbon; and he hoped, by a vigorous pursuit, to put into execution the orders of his master. He decided upon this operation.

Lord Wellington evacuated Coimbra on the approach of the enemy, upon the 1st of October; the town had generally been quitted by the higher classes of inhabitants during the preceding days; a considerable proportion, however, still remained, hoping that the enemy might yet be prevented from getting possession of it. But about ten o'clock on the morning of the first, there was suddenly an alarm that the enemy was approaching; the report was soon magnified into his having entered and at one burst the whole of the remaining inhabitants ran shrieking from the town. The bridge, which is very long and narrow, was at once choked by the crowds which were pouring upon it and the unhappy fugitives, who found their flight impeded, threw themselves into the river, and waded through it. The Mondego was fortunately not deep at this time, the dry season had kept it shallow; but there were three or four feet of water in many of the places where the unfortunate inhabitants passed it. In the midst of all the horrors of this scene; of the cries of the wretched people who were separated from their families; of those who were leaving their homes, their property, their only means of subsistence, without the prospect of procuring wherewithal to live for the next day, and of those who believed the enemy (with his train of unheard of cruelties) at their heels; the ear was most powerfully arrested by the screams of despair which issued from the gaol; where the miserable captives, who saw their countrymen escaping, believed that they should be left victims to the ferocity of the French.

The shrieks of these unhappy people were fortunately heard by Lord Wellington; who sent his *aide-de-camp*, Lord March, to relieve them from their situation; and thus the last of the inhabitants of Coimbra escaped from the enemy.

It is not in the nature of this work to dwell upon scenes of misery, such as have been now described; but the recollection of them will last long on the minds of those who witnessed them. The cruelties of the French had made an impression upon the

Portuguese, that nothing could efface; it seemed to be beyond the power of man to await the enemy's approach. The whole country fled before him; and if any of the unhappy fugitives were discovered and chased by a French soldier, they abandoned everything to which the human mind is devoted to escape from what they looked upon as more than death, the grasp of their merciless invaders.—Innumerable instances of these melancholy truths might be detailed; but it would waste the time of the reader, and the relations of the horrid acts committed by the French would be too shocking to dwell upon.

When Lord Wellington retired to Coimbra, he passed his divisions to the rear, and placed them in echelons upon the road to Leyria. As soon as he was convinced of Massena's approach, he directed each division to move one march in retreat, and he fixed his headquarters at Redinha. The cavalry which covered the army skirmished with the French in the plains of the , and obtained some advantages over those who attempted to pass the river. The following day, Lord Wellington moved to Leyria, where he remained till the enemy marched upon him.

Massena had hoped to have overtaken some part of Lord Wellington's infantry, when he advanced to Coimbra; but having failed, he pushed forward on the evening of that day to Condeixa; still he was deceived, Lord Wellington's columns were not to be overtaken; and he was obliged to halt for three days. His army was fatigued with the severe marches it had made, his provisions were exhausted; he was obliged to sack the town of Coimbra, to collect what the inhabitants had left; and he was constrained to make some arrangement for his sick and wounded, who amounted to 5,000 men, and who were too numerous to be carried with him. Massena's intercepted despatch to Bonaparte, proves how strongly he felt the difficulty of his situation. He says that he is unable to leave a guard of any strength to protect his wounded, as it would weaken his army; and that the best security he can afford them, is by pursuing the allies with the whole of his force and driving them from the country.

It is surprising, that the French officers should still have en-

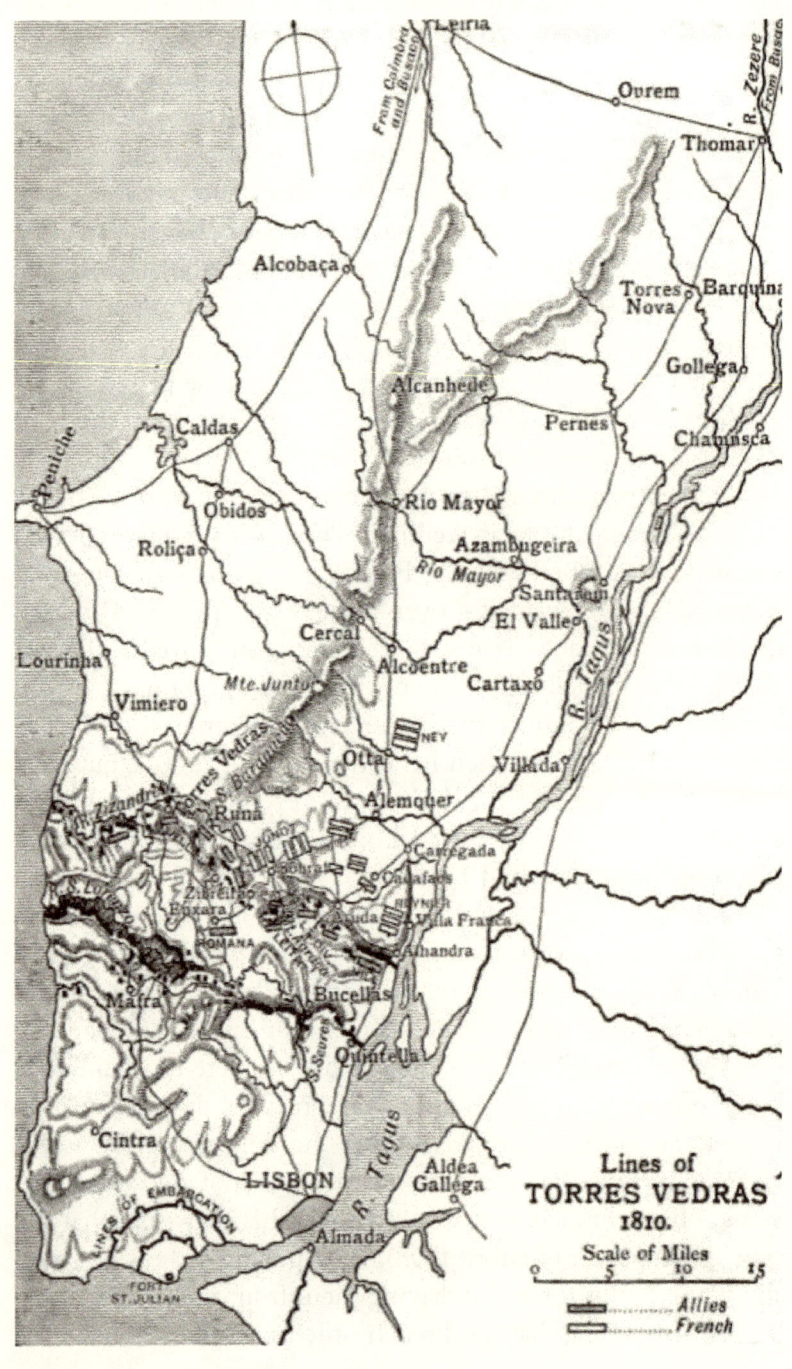

tertained this hope. In a letter from Marshal Ney to his wife, he says, that everything is going on better than could be expected, that the English are flying before the French army, and that they appear to have no other object in view than to escape to their transports, and to carry away as great a number of the youth of Portugal as they can entrap, by way of *dédommagement,* for the great expenses of the war.

On the 4th of October Massena closed his divisions to his advanced guard at Pombal, and early on the 5th pushed forward with great rapidity on Leyria, hoping to reach some part of the allied army, but he was again deceived. Lord Wellington had placed his troops in echelons to the rear, and as soon as he was apprised of the movement of the French, he directed them to fall back. The advanced guard of the British cavalry had a sharp *rencontre* with the enemy, where three French officers and a considerable number of dragoons were taken. This was the only reward Marshal Massena derived from the rapidity of his advance.

Lord Wellington moved to Alcobaca, the next day to Rio Mayor, the next to Alemquer, and on the 8th of October he entered a part of his lines at Arruda. The French army pressed forward during these days with very great exertion, but by the able arrangements of Lord Wellington it was unable to overtake any part of his troops. Several skirmishes took place between the cavalry of the two armies, they were universally in favour of the British, who closed their operations by bringing in a squadron of French. The rains set in on the 8th; the allied army did not suffer from them, as it entered its positions on the 9th, and was generally placed in villages and under cover. The French were materially annoyed by them; the roads became extremely bad; their horses, which had been short of forage, and had made some most distressing marches, were in many instances unable to get forward with the artillery; great numbers of them perished, and the troops who were without cover, suffered most severely from the inclemency of the weather.

We have thus conducted the British army to the termination of one of the most extraordinary operations which was ever carried into effect; the boldness of the original conception, as well as the perseverance and success with which it was executed will command the admiration of all military men. The ascendency which the character and talents of Lord Wellington had obtained over the minds of all those who were within his guidance or control, could alone have enabled him to effect a plan which involved in it such fearful consequences. To have persuaded a foreign government and army, but lately subjected to his direction, to abandon the greater proportion of their country, almost without a struggle, to the ravages of an invader; to see his approach to the capital without fear or hesitation, speaks of itself a confidence in the talents of the commander which is without example.

Not less extraordinary was the mode in which a movement in retreat was executed from Almeida to Torres Vedras, a distance of 150 miles, in presence of a superior army, whose object was, by every exertion in its power, to harass the corps opposed to it; yet not a straggler was overtaken, no article of baggage captured, no corps of infantry, except where the invaders were routed at Busaco, was ever seen or molested. Of all the retreats which have ever been executed, this deserves most to be admired. The steady principle on which it was carried into effect could alone have secured its success. Lord Wellington never swerved from his purpose; the various changes which every day occur in war, made no impression on his determination. The great event of a battle, such as that of Busaco, won over an enemy who was surrounded by a hostile nation, never induced him to change the plan of operations which he was convinced would in the end produce the most decisive advantages. Guided by such a principle, Lord Wellington was enabled triumphantly to execute his plan; the successes which have since attended his career are the best evidences of its wisdom.

It is a singular circumstance, that when in his turn Massena had to conduct his army in retreat over nearly the same ground to the frontiers of Spain, although he had the advantages of making his preparations in secret, and of disguising the moment of putting it into execution, yet he was constantly overtaken; the corps of his army beaten and harassed; and in every action which he was compelled to fight, he was driven with loss and disaster from his positions.

Lord Wellington placed his army on the ground marked out for it in the course of the 8th, 9th, and 10th of October. The lines, as they have been termed, extended from Alhandra to the mouth of the Zizandra; the whole distance may be computed at about twenty-five miles from right to left. The term of lines was but little applicable to them; the defences procured by art were confined to closed redoubts placed upon the most essential points, and calculated to resist, although the enemy's troops might have established themselves in their rear. They were thus enabled to protect the formation of the army upon any point attacked, before the enemy could bring cannon in operation with the troops which he might have pushed forward between them.

These forts were occupied, with very few, exceptions, not by the regular army destined to act in the field, but by the militia, of which that of Lisbon formed a part, mixed up with a certain number of troops of the line. Their defence was thus entrusted to a description of force, capable of the service imposed upon it, but which would have been of trifling assistance in a field of battle. Each redoubt was provisioned for a certain time, and was supplied with the ammunition, &c, necessary for its protracted defence. The post of Alhandra, which formed the right of the whole position, was strong by nature, and was, besides, fortified by several redoubts; its defence was assisted by the gunboats in the Tagus. The corps under the orders of Lieutenant General Hill occupied this part of the position. It defended the great approach to Lisbon, and its possession was of the greatest importance. Lieutenant General Hill communicated by his left, which was placed on the ground at the back of Arruda, on the Sierra de Monte Agraca, with the corps of the centre, which occupied the heights above Sobral. These heights, over which passed the second great road to Lisbon, having been fortified as much as the nature of the ground would admit, formed the principal point of defence on this part of the line. From this place towards the left, and in the vicinity of Ribaldiera, there were several passes into the main position, all of which were fortified; and the principal force of the army was concentrated in rear of them. The next points of importance were Runa and Undesquiera, supported by the line of heights in their rear; they were upon the road leading from Sobral to Torres Vedras, and were of the most essential consequence, since they commanded the only pass to the latter place within the Monte Junto; an advantage important to the strength of the whole position, and which never could with safety be abandoned. These posts were well fortified; were occupied by a considerable corps, and supported by the force under Major General Picton at Torres Vedras.

It is necessary to give some description of Monte Junto, which has just been mentioned, for although it was without the position, yet it was one of the main features which contributed to its general strength. This mountain runs directly north from Runa, for a distance of twelve or fourteen miles; there are no great roads or communications leading over it; the valley to the eastward, which divides it from Sobral, is impassable; it prevents, therefore, all military communication for an army from that town to Torres Vedras, excepting that stated as being occupied, but round its northern point, and thus requiring a march of at least two days. The difficulty of passing across this mountain was so great that two corps separated by it could have carried no assistance to each other, if either had been attacked. There were therefore two portions of the British position, one that might be assailed from the east of Monte Junto, the other, of which Torres Vedras was the right, and the sea at the mouth of the Zizandra the left, which might be attacked from the west. Lord Wellington's communication from one to the other of these branches of his whole position was perfectly safe and easy; and in a few hours the greater part of his troops could be transported to the defence of either;

whereas the direct contrary was the case, as has been shown, with the enemy. This formed one of the main features of the strength of the lines.

Torres Vedras and the ground about it was strongly fortified; forts were continued, at intervals, to the sea, and, although this part of the position was never menaced, yet it was occupied by garrisons, and was prepared to resist any attack that should be made. upon it.

In rear of this line of positions was a second, extending from the back of Alverca to Bucellas, thence along the Sierra di Serves and the Sierra di Barca to Montachique, from whence by the park wall of Mafra to the rear of Gradel, and along the line of heights to the mouth of the St. Lorenzo. Betwixt these two lines of positions there were strong works at Enxara di Cavalhieros, at Carasquiera, and Mattacores, covering the communication between them. To the south, and on the other side of the Tagus the heights which commanded the town and anchorage of Lisbon were also fortified, and a corps of 10,000 men, partly marines from the fleet, were destined to defend them; they extended from Almada to the fort called Bugia, opposite Fort St. Julian's. These last defences were carried into effect with a view to resisting any force the enemy might bring through the Alentejo against the capital, which at one time was menaced by the corps under Marshal Mortier, then assembled on the frontier of that province.

Massena arrived with the 6th and 8th corps of his army at Sobral on the 10th, 11th, and 12th of October. The 2nd corps followed Lieutenant General Hill upon Alhandra. These troops were considerably fatigued with the forced marches they had in vain been making to come up with Lord Wellington's army. The rain which had fallen since the 8th instant had rendered the roads extremely bad, particularly about Sobral, so that the men, and particularly the horses, were almost exhausted when they arrived in front of our positions.

Massena occupied himself the first days with reconnoitring the ground on which Lord Wellington had placed his army; the task was difficult; it was so concealed behind the hills that a very small part of it could be discovered, enough, however, was perceptible to convince him that an attack was no easy undertaking. Lord Wellington occupied a redoubt at the foot of the great height above Sobral; the French established one at a short distance and opposite to it.

After several reconnoitres, Massena determined to carry the British redoubt. The troops which occupied it were commanded by Colonel the Honourable H. Cadogan, of the 73rd Regiment. Massena placed himself on a hill to see the success of his first operation against our lines. He was disappointed, his chosen troops were repulsed, and in sight of both armies the French redoubt was carried and maintained. From this moment no event of any consequence took place for a considerable length of time. Skirmishes in the rear of the French army, and particularly from the village of Ramalhal, where the brigade of British cavalry under Major General De Grey was posted, were almost the only military events which took place. These were chiefly brought about by parties of the French, who, in search of provisions, were continually met by Lord Wellington's patrols, and in which a number of prisoners were taken.

It is of consequence here to take a general view of the situation in which the French army was placed. Massena, when he entered Portugal, commanded a force of 72,000 effective men. The plan of operations he adopted was to break in at once upon Lord Wellington's defences, to pursue him till he forced him to a battle, to allow no circumstances to arrest this decision and finish thus at one blow the campaign entrusted to his conduct. In pursuance of his system he marched, with all the corps of his army concentrated, into the heart of Portugal, taking his line direct upon Coimbra, at which place, by turning Lord Wellington's left, he hoped to have arrived almost without resistance. In effecting this movement, he left no garrisons behind him; he occupied no posts to secure even his communication with Spain, or to ensure him any supplies or protection from the rear of his army. Such considerations were all sacrificed to preserve his greater numerical force for the battle by which he hoped at once to decide the fate of Portugal. The first interruption to this arrangement of the campaign, was the assembling of the whole British army at Busaco, and the subsequent defeat of the French.

On the day on which this took place, Massena's communication with Spain was cut off by a force of Portuguese militia upon the frontiers near Pinhel and Celorico. He determined, however, to continue his original movement and, hoping to conceal his march through the Sierra of Caramula, expected again to turn Lord Wellington, and fight a battle to advantage in the open country between Busaco and Coimbra. These hopes were frustrated. Perceiving the difficulties into which the enemy was plunging, Lord Wellington retired through Coimbra, and abandoned to him that deserted town and country. Arrived at this point, Marshal Massena must have begun to feel the difficulties of his situation. He was encumbered with 5,000 wounded from the battle of Busaco, he was without the security of any supply of provisions in the midst of a most inimical and exasperated population; he was without the means of communicating with Spain. If he remained where he was, the boasted conquest of Portugal in a campaign was at an end; the difficulties to which he must have exposed himself, by the extension of his army to procure provisions, must also have had weight with him; and the uncertainty as to our real object in so rapid a retreat, must have induced him to expect some great result from the bolder measure of pursuing the allied army. In conformity to this feeling, without leaving any protection for his rear, or even for his wounded, Marshal Massena conducted his army to Sobral. His progress here was totally arrested.

The strength of the position occupied by us was such, as, with the recollection of Busaco fresh upon him, Massena dared not attack; he was, therefore, reduced at once to the defensive, his mighty vengeance was conducted harmless to this unpromising position.

The first news, which must have been unpleasant to Marshal Massena, was the capture of Coimbra, with all the French wounded, by a corps of Portuguese militia under Colonel Trant. The loss of the troops was not alone to be lamented in this case; it brought with it the disastrous conviction that the French army was insulated on the ground on which it stood; no line of communication, no extent of country in subjection, from which to draw resources, remained to it. Wherever a Frenchman stood, for the moment, he commanded and desolated the spot, removed from it all was in hostility against him. The march of the French, through Portugal to the lines, was most singular. The troops seldom saw an inhabitant, they could procure no guides, deserters from them, or prisoners, could never state the towns or villages from whence they came, though, in some instances, they had been weeks in the same places; they had seen no native to instruct them in their names. In this state of things, the French army began early to suffer from privations of every sort; its foraging parties were scouring the country in the rear, and upon their success depended chiefly the provisioning of the troops. The fatigue and sickness, consequent on this mode of living, were considerable.

The French soldiers were generally bivouaced along the line they occupied, which, without shelter in the rainy season, increased the misery of their situation. By these causes, their army gradually diminished; while, on the contrary, that under Lord Wellington, excellently provided with all that was necessary; and mostly under cover in the villages within the position, was gaining strength and improving in discipline every day. The Spanish corps, under the orders of the Marquis of Romana, had joined the allied army from the frontiers of Estremadura, so that the force at this time, the end of October and beginning of November, within the lines, was considerably greater than that of the enemy. Under these circumstances, Lord Wellington saw there was an opportunity of attacking Massena with advantage. The problem, whether it were wise to do so or not, engaged his most serious attention. He was persuaded, that if he attacked, he could secure a victory; to attempt it he was induced by every personal consideration, the glory which would have accrued to him in success would at that time have been immense, in England the word of Bonaparte, that his eagles should be planted on the towers of Lisbon, was generally looked upon as a decree which no talent or ability could avert. To have learnt at such a time that our army had defeated the boasted instruments of this prophesying emperor, would have carried the man who executed such a plan to the pinnacle of greatness. Yet this inducement, as well as the anxious wish of the whole army to attack, had no effect. Lord Wellington was persuaded that the sounder line of conduct was to wait with patience, and in safety, the mischief which he was satisfied would be brought upon the enemy by want and sickness, and by the continual hostility of the natives. He therefore decided steadily to pursue that plan; he was ever watchful to profit by any advantage which should be afforded, but unless a decided one was given him, he determined to remain on the defensive.

About the beginning of November, Massena found his sick so fast increasing, and his means of obtaining provisions so much diminished, that he was obliged to detach General La Bordes division of the 6th corps, to form a garrison at Santarem for the protection of an hospital, as well as to assist the foraging parties in that quarter.

Lord Wellington made a corresponding movement to prevent the passage of the Tagus, by detaching Major General Fane with a brigade of cavalry into the Alemtejo to assemble opposite to La Borde. In this situation the armies remained in perfect tranquillity till the 15th in the morning, when it was found that during the night the whole French army had retreated. This movement had been carried into effect in such silence, that no suspicion of it had been entertained.

It was the great triumph of Lord Wellington's skill and foresight, that, without exposing a single man in action, he had since the 10th of October retained at first a superior army in inactivity before him; he had seen it diminish in numbers every day; and, in the end, without its having effected a single purpose, he had obliged it to retire, oppressed with fatigue and sickness.

Towards reducing the country it occupied, it had not made the slightest progress. The provisions of the British army were drawn from the northern provinces in its rear; Coimbra continued occupied by the Portuguese militia; Abrantes by the Portuguese garrison; so that it may truly be described as commanding only the ground on which it stood.

The state of Lisbon during the period when the enemy was hardly twenty miles distant from it, deserves to be mentioned. Massena had expected that his near approach would have caused tumult and a revolution; but far from this, as a proof of the extraordinary confidence entertained of Lord Wellington, no town was ever in more perfect quiet; there never appeared in it the slightest symptom of fear or apprehension. The ordinary occupations were continued, although the enemy was but a single march from it. Yet total ruin was known to await the town if Massena, by succeeding against the allied army, forced an entry into it. The apprehension of such a catastrophe was, however, at no time entertained; implicit reliance on the skill of their chief, and the bravery of the troops, was the universal sentiment of the Portuguese.

The persons whose property had been surrendered to be laid waste by the enemy, showed the same feelings; the poor peasants, who had abandoned everything they possessed, were alike persuaded that all was done for the best; and in the whole country there was not a dissenting voice in giving unlimited confidence to Lord Wellington.

CHAPTER 13

Massena in Retreat

As soon as the retreat of the enemy was known, the allied army was put in motion to follow him; his movement was, however, so rapid, that he was not overtaken till within a few miles of Santarem. The rearguard was pushed over the bridge in front of that place, where it took up a strong and formidable position.

Lord Wellington had not pursued the enemy with the whole of his force; suspecting, that it might, in the first instance, be the intention of Massena to move round Monte Junto, he retained Major General Picton's division in its position at Torres Vedras; he afterwards detached Lieutenant General Hill with the corps under his orders across the Tagus at Valada, with a view of communicating with Abrantes, which it might be the intention of the French to attack, and also to protect the Alemtejo from any offensive operation.

The rest of the army was brought opposite to Santarem. Lord Wellington, having received a report from Major General Fane that the baggage of the French army was retiring towards Thomar, conceived that Massena was altogether falling back; with this idea he determined to attack what appeared to be his rearguard, which was placed upon a small river, the Rio Mayor. A disposition with this view was made; a part of Brigadier General Pack's brigade was to have passed, supported by a detachment of cavalry, on the right of the French position, about a mile beyond it; Sir William Erskine's brigade supported by the Guards, was to have stormed the bridge; while Major General Crawford, with the light division, was to have attacked the enemy's left, and along the Tagus to have menaced the rear of his advanced position. The rain, which had been very heavy during the preceding days, had, however, so much swelled the river where Brigadier General Pack was to have passed, that it was found impracticable; the enemy also appearing in considerable force, the operation was given up. Lord Wellington still determining to adhere to his defensive system, and deciding rather to fall back again upon his lines than seek the French army, or give it an opportunity of meeting him upon any thing like equal terms.

Massena continued the succeeding days to strengthen his position at Santarem; Lord Wellington retained only his light division in front of it, and placed the rest of his army in echelons to the rear. The headquarters were placed at Cartaxo; Sir Brent Spencer, with the Guards and Major General Cameron's brigade, in the same place; Lieutenant General Cole's division at Azambujo, Major General Leith's at Alcoentre, Major General A. Campbell's at Alemquer, Major General Picton's at Torres Vedras and the Spaniards at Villa-Franca.

Massena threw a bridge over the Zezere at its confluence with the Tagus, as if with the intention of passing a corps for the siege of Abrantes; he was contented, however, with reconnoitring that place, which he never after molested. He placed his army in cantonments stretching as far back as Thomar, Torres Novas, and Alcanede; and in this situation, protected by the position at Santarem, remained in quiet, apparently awaiting reinforcements and orders how to proceed.

Lord Wellington saw this with perfect indifference; he was persuaded that the more the enemy was reinforced the greater would be his suffering, and the less the general advantage to his cause in the Peninsula. He determined, therefore, to undertake no operation to prevent it, nor any other which could either cause him risk, or could draw him from his general system of defensive measures.

From this period, the 12th of November 1810, to the 4th of March, 1811, both armies retained their respective positions.

The only events of any importance, were the arrival of the 9th corps of 10,000 men, commanded by General Cte. Erlon, which was placed by Massena to protect his right at Leiria, and the junction of 5,000 men, who were brought by General Foy upon his return from Paris, where he had been sent by Massena, soon after his arrival opposite our lines, to render an account of the operations of the French army, and of its situation. Bonaparte received the relation of these events with much indifference; and observed upon the excuses General Foy was directed to make, for the loss of the battle of Busaco, *"Ah bah! les Anglais de tout temps ont battu les Francais."*

General Gardane, in attempting to carry a corps of 3,000 men to join Massena, was driven back by some Portuguese militia. General Claparede posted himself, with a corps of 8,000 men, in the environs of Guarda; from whence he had several actions with the irregulars in that part of the country, by whom the communication of the French army with Spain had been totally cut off.

During the whole of this period, the French subsisted solely on the plunder of the country they occupied. The irregular manner in which this mode of obtaining supplies was conducted, led to the perpetration of the most revolting atrocities. Torture inflicted upon the inhabitants, to extract from them the secret of their depots of provisions and property, was one of the expedients most common to the French soldiery. The murder of the peasantry seemed. to be committed without remorse; the capture of the women was converted often into a source of profit. Nothing more revolting to the mind of civilized man can be produced, than the list of horrors committed during this lamentable period.

Bonaparte directed Massena to continue his occupation of Portugal, till he could operate, with Marshals Mortier and Soult, to whom he had given orders to advance into the Alemtejo, and thence combine their movements for an attack on Lord Wellington. In conformity with these views, Marshal Mortier arrived in the beginning of January in Spanish Estremadura; he soon after captured Olivenza, and laid siege to Badajos. Lord Wellington, upon the first notice of these movements, had detached the Spanish corps which had joined him in the lines, to reinforce the corps of General Mendizabel, which was already destined to the protection of these places; he at the same time strongly recommended that officer not to fight a battle, but, by taking up a defensive position, which he pointed out to him, to give every assistance to the defence of Badajos, and the other fortresses in that quarter.

Unfortunately for Spain, for the interests of the allies, and for those persons who, acquainted with the Marquis of Romana, loved and cherished him for the virtues which adorned his character, he had expired in the beginning of January at Cartaxo; less able hands were now entrusted with the army he had commanded.

On the 19th of January, General Mendizabel was attacked in a position close to Badajos by the French army which was besieging it, and totally defeated. Mortier, from that moment, pushed on without interruption the operations of the siege. The place surrendered on the 11th of March, notwithstanding the governor was informed by telegraph that a strong corps of the allied army was coming to his relief, and that Massena was already on his retreat from Santarem. It is a fact worthy of remark, that, in the articles of capitulation for this place, it was stipulated that the garrison should march out by the breach; but when this came to be examined, it was found so far from practicable, that it was necessary to employ some time to make it fit for the passage of the troops. The garrison was stronger than the corps which besieged it; so that taking all the circumstances into consideration, the giving up this important fortress was as extraordinary as it was disastrous.

Throughout the month of February, Lord Wellington had been looking out with great anxiety for a reinforcement from England, which was coming to him, and which, by the unfavourable state of the weather, had been unusually delayed, and did not arrive till the 7th of March. The distressed state of the French army, as well as the menaced movement of Soult and

Mortier, had determined him, upon the arrival of this reinforcement, which amounted to 7,000 English, to attack; and his plans for this purpose were already decided upon.

The night of the 4th of March, however, put an end to this project. Massena broke up from all his positions, and commenced his retreat. The country he had occupied was totally exhausted; his army could no longer subsist in it. The sickness and misery the French had suffered, together with the hostility of the peasants, had considerably reduced their numbers. Lord Wellington had triumphed in his calculations without the loss of a single man, he had obliged the enemy, weakened and disheartened, to abandon all his objects.

Massena, after having previously moved off his sick and baggage upon the road to the Peunte de Marcella, directed his effective army upon Pombal, where it appeared he had intended to fight a battle; some altercation is stated to have taken place here, between him and the Count Erlon, that officer having received instructions to act in Spain, insisted upon being allowed to retire from Portugal, and immediately commenced his movement to effect that object.

Lord Wellington had on the 11th, concentrated a part of his army opposite Pombal; the enemy was driven from it, and the next day was attacked at Redinha, from, the positions about which place he was also obliged to retire with considerable loss: from thence he was pushed upon Condeixa, where, appearing to take up his ground as if to defend it, Lord Wellington instantly detached a corps to menace his left, and his communication with Miranda do Corvo. This had the desired effect; Marshal Ney, who commanded the French rearguard, retired upon Miranda, thus abandoning the chance of occupying Coimbra, which was without defence, or of retaining any advanced position in Portugal.

To the activity and vigour with which Lord Wellington pushed the French army, this advantage was entirely due. Massena conceived that an officer who for so long a period had acted with so much caution, would never seriously venture to disturb his retreat. He had therefore, relied upon being able to conduct it at his own discretion: when he found, on the contrary, that he was most vigorously attacked, he was obliged to precipitate his movements. To this alone can be attributed his having been unable to ascertain that there was no garrison in Coimbra, a position to which it appears he was anxious to have led his army.

Lord Wellington pursued the enemy, and obliged him precipitately to abandon Miranda do Corvo, leaving a great part of his baggage, and destroying, at Foz d'Arouse, a considerable number of his carts and baggage-horses. Ney took up a position on the Ciera; but having left a considerable part of his advanced guard on the left bank of that river, it was vigorously attacked by the allies, and in complete disorder and with great loss was driven into the. main position. A French eagle was taken in the river, into which, in the hurry of defeat, a. considerable number of the enemy had been precipitated, and drowned.

On the 17th, Massena formed his army in a strong position behind the Alva, occupying the Puente de Marcella, and the heights along the banks of that river. Believing himself secure in this formidable position, he had sent out detachments from the different corps, to collect provisions; but Lord Wellington passed the Alva on the left of the French army, and obliged it to retire without having reassembled the parties sent out to forage, a considerable number of which were taken.

The whole of these operations were conducted with the most transcendent skill and ability. Whenever the enemy halted to defend himself he was out-manoeuvred, and driven from his ground; he was constantly attacked and beaten. Besides the loss in battle, his stragglers, his sick and wounded, and a considerable part of his baggage, became a prey to the allied army.

Lord Wellington was now obliged, for a moment, to give up the active pursuit he had hitherto maintained. His army had out-marched its supplies; he was forced to give time for them to join him; he had besides been obliged to detach a considerable force into the Alemtejo, which, having reduced his numbers below those of the enemy, forced him to proceed with caution.

When Massena commenced his retreat, Lord Wellington had decided to send the second, British division, together with that of General Hamilton of Portuguese, with the 13th Light Dragoons, and a Portuguese brigade of cavalry, to protect the Alemtejo, and to oblige Mortier to raise the siege of Badajos; a part of this corps having, however, passed to the north of the Tagus at Abrantes, and driven the enemy from the Zezere at Punhete, its march to the southward was delayed till Lord Wellington, receiving intelligence of the surrender of Badajos, was obliged to add to this force the 4th division, under Lieutenant-General Cole, and the heavy brigade of British cavalry, under Major-General De Grey. This immense detachment from his army, was rendered necessary from, the very great importance of defending the southern frontier of Portugal, while the, remainder of his forces pursued the enemy in the north. It was entrusted to the command of Marshal Beresford, and began its march towards Portalegre and Campo Mayor on the 17th. Lord Wellington considered the possession of Badajos as of the greatest importance to his future operations; and therefore directed Marshal Beresford, if possible, to invest it before the enemy should have had time to repair the fortifications, and provision it.. This object was unfortunately not accomplished and the recapture of that fortress, at a later period, was most dearly purchased.

After a few days' halt upon the Alva, the allied troops continued the pursuit of Massena's army; it had taken a position at Guarda, where it appeared determined to defend itself. The ground about that town is extremely strong; being at a considerable height, it commands the country around it, and is most difficult of access. Massena had availed himself of these advantages, and hoped to maintain his army, protected by them, within the frontier of Portugal. He had held out this hope to Bonaparte, and therefore made every disposition within his means to secure his object; but Lord Wellington, on the 27th, in the morning, had manoeuvred with seven columns, so as to turn him on every side, and having gained possession of his position, to force him to a precipitate retreat. A brigade of French infantry; under General Maucune, was near being taken, and the whole French army was driven across the Coa. Massena here made a last effort to maintain some footing within the frontiers of the country, of which he had so triumphantly predicted the entire conquest; he placed his army along the Coa, and in occupation of Sabugal. He was attacked, however, on the 2nd of April, his hopes were blasted, he was driven into Spain. Lord Wellington had directed the light division to pass, the Coa on the left, and in rear of General Regnier's corps, while two divisions attacked in front. From the badness of the weather, a battalion of the Rifle Corps, under Colonel Beckwith, was deceived in the ford at which it was to cross, and got engaged alone for a considerable time with almost the whole of the French force. Colonel Beckwith, at the moment of being charged by the French cavalry, took advantage of a stone enclosure, from whence he defended himself with the most distinguished gallantry. An opportunity offering, he charged and took a howitzer, which he maintained, and, after having caused a severe loss to the enemy, was relieved by the arrival of the rest of the light division, and afterwards of the other corps which had been destined to the attack. Regnier was obliged to retire with great precipitation, leaving a considerable number of killed and wounded, and losing many prisoners on his march to Alfaiates, where he entered the Spanish territory.

Thus were the last of Massena's troops chased from the country of which they still maintained the pompous appellation. "The Army of Portugal," was yet the title they were distinguished by, though they could boast of that country but as the scene of disaster and defeat; and out of which, with the loss of half their numbers, they had been driven headlong, leaving only the sad remembrance of the atrocities they had committed.

Lord Wellington having reconnoitred Almeida, decided immediately to blockade it, having appointed the corps for that purpose and distributed the rest of his army in cantonments, he went to the Alemtejo, to visit the army commanded by

Marshal Beresford. This force had arrived at Campo Mayor on the 25th of March, the town had, two days before, after a spirited resistance, surrendered to the enemy, but the wretched state of its defences obliged Marshal Mortier to abandon it on the approach of the allies. The advanced-guard, composed of the 13th Light Dragoons, and some Portuguese cavalry, came up with the enemy's convoy, protected by a corps of cavalry, three, battalions of infantry and a brigade of artillery, as it was: retiring to Badajos. Colonel Head charged the French cavalry, defeated it, and drove it to the gates of Badajos, from the walls of which place the 13th Light Dragoons suffered some loss, having, in the ardour of the pursuit, exposed themselves to the fire from them.

The heavy brigade of British cavalry, composed of the 3rd Dragoon Guards and the 4th Dragoons, came up to the French infantry soon after this charge had taken place, but at the moment of attacking it, were halted by Marshal Beresford, who, in doubt of the event of the charge made by the 13th, did not venture to expose the rest of his cavalry to any risk. This infantry therefore was allowed to move off without molestation, and in the night the French were enabled to carry into Badajos a great part of the guns, stores, and ammunition, which, in the charge of the 13th Dragoons, had been taken in the morning. The result of this affair, after so brilliant a commencement, was unfortunate. The return of the infantry was a considerable reinforcement to a garrison we were about to attack and the artillery, stores, and provisions were objects of the first necessity to its defence.

The French having thus been driven over the Guadiana, Marshal Beresford sought as early as possible to pass that river, to invest Badajos according to the instructions he had received. He was delayed, however; by the state of the river, and his unwillingness to risk its passage, without having previously secured his after communications across it; so that he did not effectually establish himself on the left bank, till the 6th and 7th of April, by which time the enemy had provisioned and repaired the place, and Marshal Mortier, leaving it in a state of defence, had retired with his corps towards Seville.

The blockade of Badajos was immediately established; and Lieutenant-General Cole was directed to conduct the siege of Olivenza, which, having only a garrison of 370 men, was surrendered at discretion on the 15th.

Chapter 14
Albuhera & Fuentes d'Honor

Immediately after this event, and while Marshal Beresford was preparing for the attack of Badajos, Lord Wellington arrived. He was strongly impressed with the importance of this fortress to his future plans, in the new system of warfare which the late events had laid open to him. Snatched from him at the moment all his other calculations had triumphed, it had already been most detrimental to his general success. By the large detachment he had been obliged to make from his army, in consequence of its fall, it had prevented his more vigorous pursuit of Massena, and had destroyed his hope of undertaking the blockade of Ciudad Rodrigo, as well as that of Almeida, before it could be re-victualled, and placed in a state of defence; and it still menaced, as long as it remained in the hands of the French, to curb all his offensive movements into Spain by protecting their positions in the south of the country and by enabling them at all times to threaten the southern provinces of Portugal.

Lord Wellington found the army of Marshal Beresford in possession of the whole of Estremadura. An affair of cavalry which had taken place at Usagre, in which the 3rd Dragoon Guards had most gallantly charged and defeated the French, had, terminated their attempt to maintain themselves within it. Lord Wellington immediately reconnoitred Badajos with two battalions of infantry and some Portuguese cavalry; a sharp affair was engaged, by these troops with part of the garrison, but he effected his purpose, and decided to besiege the place, and fixed upon such points to, attack as he hoped would lead to the capture of the fortress within fourteen or sixteen days. He had neither the means nor the time to undertake a regular siege; besieging artillery, stores, and ammunition could all be but very, inefficiently supplied from Elvas, the only depot from whence they could be drawn and it was evident that Soult would make every effort to prevent the capture of the place and that he would, in about three weeks, be able to collect an army strong enough to attempt its relief.

The heights of St. Christobal, on the right of the Guadiana, seemed to offer a favourable emplacement for the, establishment of batteries to protect an attack on the old castle; it was therefore decided to carry, if possible, the fort which occupied them, and afterwards, from that position, to endeavour to destroy the defences of the castle, while its walls should be breached from the batteries in the plain below, and on the left of the river. Preparations were immediately made to carry this plan into effect, which Lord Wellington hoped would be in operation on the 24th. The movements of Massena recalled him to the north; he therefore left the prosecution of the siege to Marshal Beresford, recommending, if the enemy attempted to disturb him, to fight a battle, rather than be driven from his object.

The commencement of the siege was most unfortunately delayed by the swelling of the Guadiana on the 24th and the consequent destruction of the bridge across it, till the 8th of May, when Major-General Lumley completed the investment on the right of that river, Major-General Sir W. Stewart having previously effected it on the left. The means provided for the siege were found very unequal to the undertaking. Before. any progress could be made, Marshal Soult had collected his army as had been anticipated. On the night of the 15th, the attack of the place was discontinued, and the troops marched to Albuhera, where, on the 16th, Marshal Beresford obtained a signal victory over the French army.

Lord Wellington returned to his headquarters at Villa Formoso on the 28th of April. Massena had collected his army at

Ciudad Rodrigo; it consisted of the 2nd, 6th, 8th, and 9th corps, with the cavalry and artillery which belonged to them, and of 1,500 cavalry of the Imperial Guard, commanded by the Duke of Istria. The whole force amounted to 40,000 men. The remnant of the army of Portugal, which, six months before, had counted above 90,000 rank and file.

Lord Wellington saw the approach of the enemy without dismay, the French force was superior to his own—its object, the relief of Almeida. To thwart this attempt it was necessary to accept a battle and, from the situation of Almeida, on the right of the Coa, the position to defend the approach to it must necessarily be taken up in front of the town, thus having the river in rear of the allied army. The banks of the Coa are extremely steep, there are few fords at which it can be passed, none in the part of it near Almeida serviceable for an army. The bridge over it, under the guns of that fortress, is extremely narrow, and at the time was nearly impassable. The bridge at Castel de Bom was also a most difficult communication. From Ciudad Rodrigo a road leads to Sabugal, where there is another bridge over the Coa, which, in case of defeat, might have served the allied army to retire over.

Lord Wellington, though not entirely from his own conviction, determined to take up a defensive position, covering both the approach to Almeida, and the road to Sabugal. He perceived, from the beginning, that this double object was more than the forces he had with him might be able to maintain. The extension to the road above mentioned weakened his position, whereas, he was persuaded that, by confining himself to the protection of Almeida alone, he could bid defiance to the enemy. The object, however, of defending the entry by Sabugal into Portugal, and of securing a second road to retire upon, was not without mature consideration to be given up and Lord Wellington felt convinced that if the necessity of so doing should arise, he could always withdraw his army to the more concentrated position.

With these views Lord Wellington took up the ground along

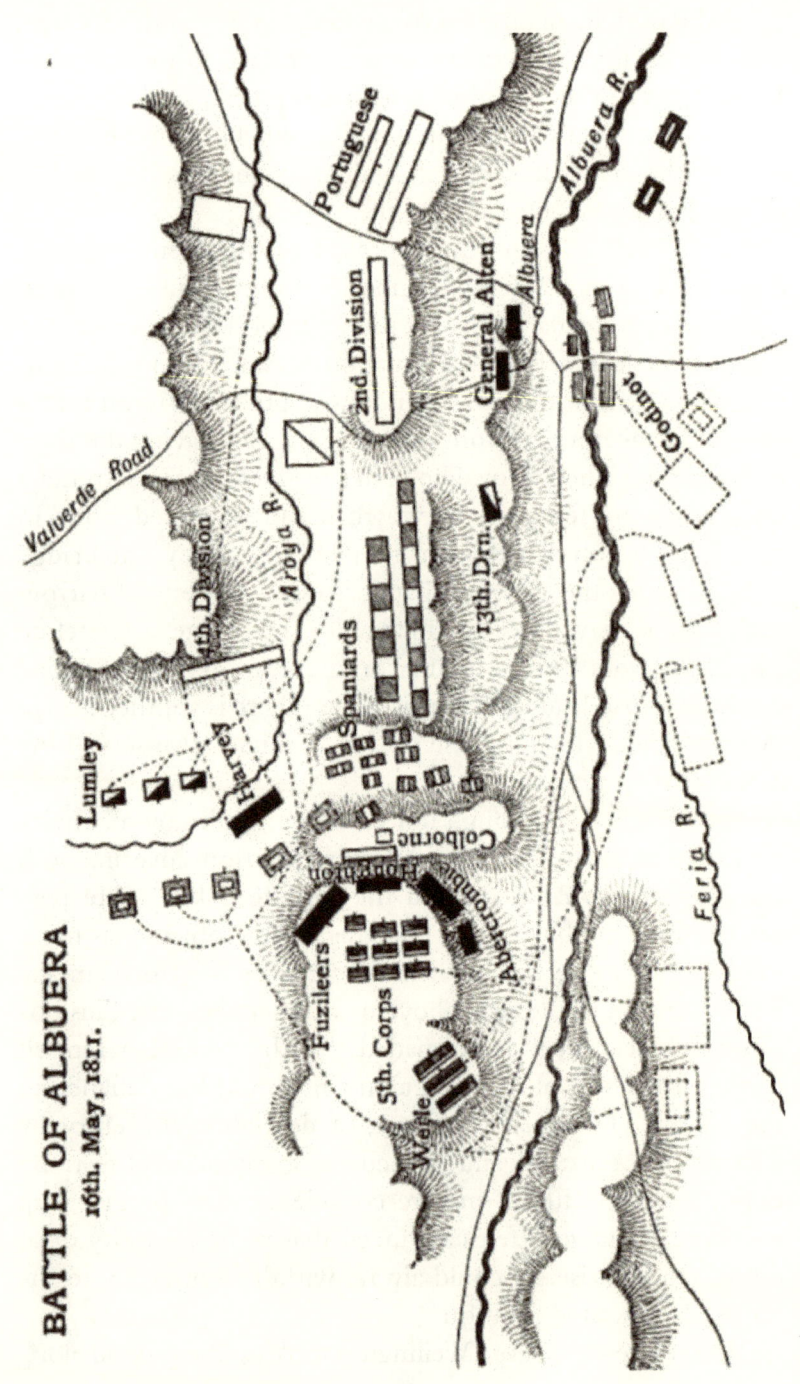

the Duas Casas. He placed the fifth division on his extreme left, near the fort of La Conception, to defend the great road to Almeida, which crosses the river at a ford immediately in front of that fortification. The light and sixth divisions he placed; opposite to, the village of Almada; the first, third, and seventh, were placed in rear of Fuentes d'Honor, with the light infantry of the third division and of the brigades of Major-Generals Nightingale and Howard occupying the village, supported by a battalion of the German Legion, the 2nd battalion of the 83rd, and the 71st and 79th Regiments. A Spanish corps, under Don Julian Sanchez, was posted on the extreme right, at Nava d'Aver. Brigadier-General, Pack, with, a brigade of Portuguese infantry and the 2nd British or Queen's Regiment, blockaded Almeida.

Massena advanced from Ciudad Rodrigo on the 2nd of May and our troops having retired from the Agueda, he arrived, on the 3rd, opposite to the position occupied by the allied army. In the evening he made a desperate attempt to carry the village of Fuentes d'Honor, but after a severe contest, most gallantly, maintained, his troops were totally repulsed. Defeated with considerable loss in his first attempt he spent the whole of the 4th in reconnoitring our position. Lord Wellington penetrated his intention of attacking the right of the allied army, and in the night moved the seventh division to Porco Velho, the only ford at which the enemy could cross the Duas Casas and where the banks of that river opposed but a trifling obstacle to his advance.

On the morning of the 5th, the eighth corps was discovered opposite to this village, and preparing to attack it. Lord Wellington moved the: light division to support the seventh, while he directed the first and third divisions to occupy some high ground between the Turon and Duas Casas rivers, thus observing the sixth and ninth corps of the French army, which had made a movement to their left, and had approached the ground occupied by the eighth corps.

Massena began the action of this day by an attack on the advanced guard of the seventh division, which, overpowered by numbers, was obliged to retire, giving up the village of Porco

Velho. The French cavalry, under General Montbrun, which had already driven Don Julian Sanches from Nava d'Aver, charged with a very superior force the cavalry of the allies, and though, in the first *rencontre*, its advance was driven back, yet it afterwards succeeded in penetrating to the infantry, which, supported in the most gallant manner by the artillery, received the French cavalry and repulsed it with considerable loss. At this moment Lord Wellington decided to withdraw his army into the more concentrated position, to which from the beginning he had felt inclined to confine himself.

He directed the light and seventh divisions, supported by the cavalry, to retire and to take up the ground extending from the Duas Casas towards Frenada, on the Coa. This movement, as bold as it was decisive, was executed with the greatest precision; the enemy could make no impression on the allied columns while on their march and the new position, at right-angles with the old one, was taken up with perfect regularity. Massena declined making any attempt on the troops now formed on their new alignment; he confined his efforts for the remainder of the day to successive attacks, made by the sixth corps, upon Fuentes d'Honor. The contest was most severe in this quarter, and lasted till night, when, with great loss on both sides, the allied troops, having completely repulsed the enemy, retained possession of this most obstinately disputed village.

So terminated this memorable action, the only one throughout the whole war in which the enemy had to boast of a momentary success against the allies. The ground at Porco Velho, from which the advance of the seventh division was obliged to retire, afforded no decisive position, and if the French infantry had been attacking at the moment of the charge of cavalry under General Montbrun, our loss in the retreat to the new alignment might have been considerably greater. Not such, however, as the French officers assert; the novelty of an advantage to them was so great, that on our change of position they predicted the entire destruction of the allied army; and although these hopes were so blasted, that they dared not afterwards make a single movement in attack upon us, yet they still persuaded themselves, that if the proper moment had been seized, we were in total confusion, and must inevitably have been defeated.

The British army can seldom be calculated upon to verify such predictions; if the French had attempted to pursue, they would, as on other occasions of the same nature, have had more to repent than to boast of. The message of General Foy to Bonaparte, before the action of Waterloo, that in the whole war in the Peninsula, the French had never once beaten the British infantry, would have been as true in its application to any attack made at the moment above alluded to, as it proved to be in the tremendous battle of Mont Saint Jean.

Defeated in all his projects, Massena, on the morning of the 6th, withdrew his troops from the front of the allied position, and, having given up all hope of forcing his way to Almeida, confined his views to a simple communication with the place, directing General Brenier to evacuate and destroy it. The French army remained in a position opposite the allies till the 10th, when it retired to Ciudad Rodrigo. Lord Wellington had employed the time since the battle of the 5th, in entrenching his new position, and had rendered it so strong that the enemy did not make any attempt against it. Marshal Marmont arrived on the 7th, and soon after superseded Marshal Massena in his command.

As soon as the French army had retired, Lord Wellington made arrangements to secure Almeida. Aware of the distressed situation of that place, he detached General Campbell, on the 10th, to resume the blockade, and to relieve Brigadier-General Pack. In the night of the same day, however, at 11 o'clock, General Brenier, having previously destroyed the defences of the place, marched out at the head of his garrison, and, taking the road to Barba del Puerco, forced his way through the pickets of the allies, and with the loss of not more than 200 men escaped to the French army. There were a variety of circumstances which favoured this undertaking. The order for the march of the 4th Regiment upon Almeida had been delayed by Sir W. Erskine; the 2nd Queen's Regiment, not believing the enemy had

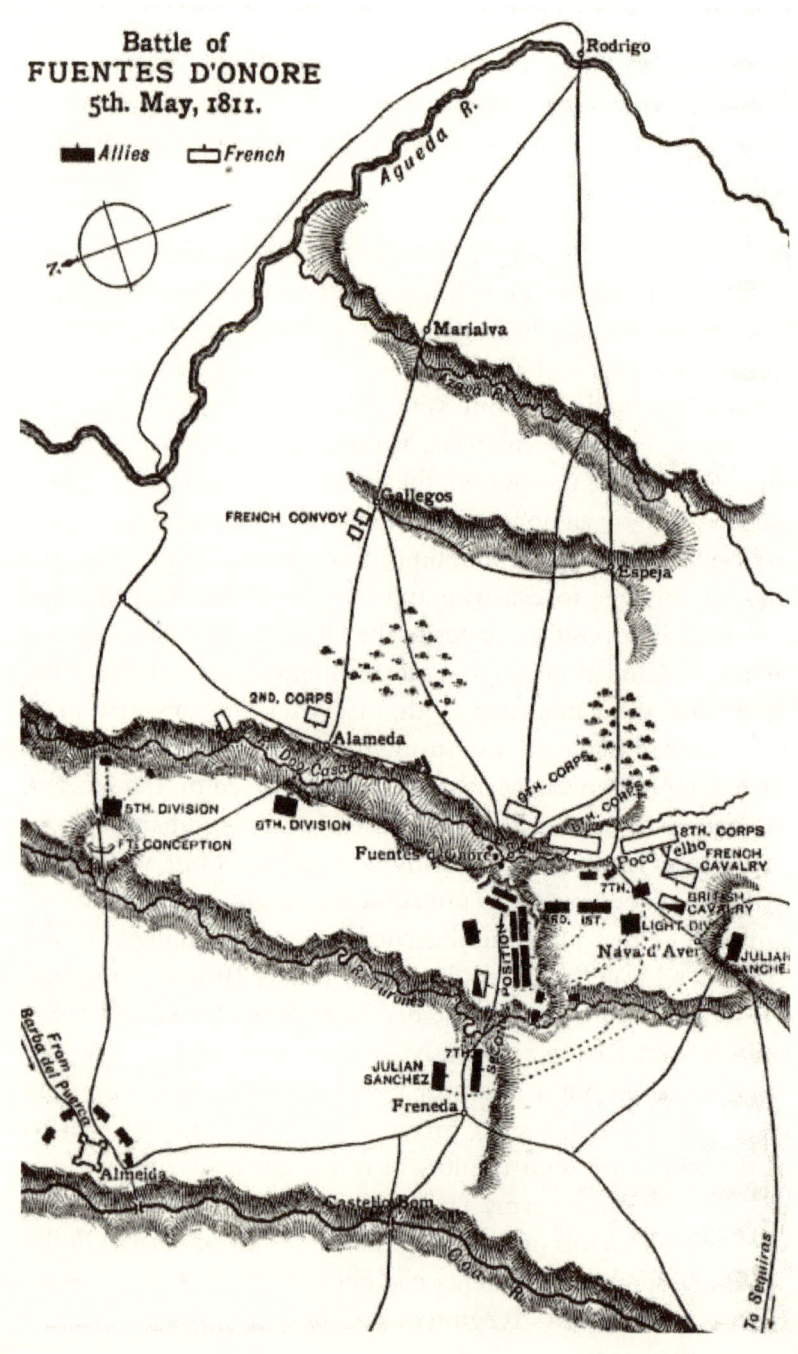

escaped, remained on their position; the orderly drummer of the 36th Regiment was not at General Campbell's quarters to give the alarm, and this regiment did not, in consequence, overtake the enemy so soon as it otherwise might have done. Brigadier General Pack, having been relieved by General Campbell, had gone from his quarters, and, during his absence, Colonel Campbell had marched his brigade to more distant villages. When Brigadier General Pack returned, he found General Campbell in possession of the house he had occupied, but as it was 9 o'clock he remained there for the night; he joined the pickets of his brigade, which were still on duty, on the first alarm, and at the point where the enemy had forced the chain. He immediately pursued with from 30 to 40 men, but this force was totally insufficient to give any serious, disturbance to the enemy. The 4th and 36th Regiments did not arrive at Barba del Puerco till daylight: at this moment Bremer was passing the bridge, and immediately afterwards joined the French corps which was stationed there to receive him.

By this event the operations in Portugal were brought to a close; that country was delivered from the enemy, and was freed forever after from his odious oppression.

The glorious and transcendent services of Lord Wellington were duly appreciated throughout the kingdom; his name was blest, and to the latest posterity will be handed down in that country with grateful recollection. He was hailed as one to whom a whole people owed their emancipation. The governors vied with the governed in expressing to him their admiration of the exalted achievements which had immortalized his name, and which had sustained the honour of the combined armies.

Lord Wellington, immediately after the capture of Almeida, detached two divisions to the southern army, and soon after proceeded himself to join Marshal Beresford.

He arrived at his headquarters after the battle of Albuhera had been fought, and as soon as the means could be collected, commenced a second time the siege of Badajos. The detail of these events which followed the deliverance of Portugal, does not, however, belong to the present work. To describe the capture of the important fortresses of Ciudad Rodrigo and Badajos, in the face of superior armies, and the destruction of that of Almaraz, by which the armies of Marmont and Soult were connected; to follow Lord Wellington through the brilliant operations which led to the battle of Salamanca, and to the reconquest of Madrid and all the southern provinces of Spain; to trace the execution of that magnificent movement, by which, all the French defences in the northern provinces of Spain being turned without a blow, their armies were completely overthrown, with the loss of all their cannon and baggage, at the battle of Vittoria, and Spain, like Portugal, was delivered from foreign rule—these glorious transactions must be left to others to record. They will be handed down, with the rest of those great events which have distinguished the triumphant career of Lord Wellington, as a beacon to guide hereafter all military men in the pursuit of fame, combined with justice, with moderation, and with virtue.

ALSO FROM LEONAUR
AVAILABLE IN SOFTCOVER OR HARDCOVER WITH DUST JACKET

A HISTORY OF THE FRENCH & INDIAN WAR *by Arthur G. Bradley*—The Seven Years War as it was fought in the New World has always fascinated students of military history—here is the story of that confrontation.

WASHINGTON'S EARLY CAMPAIGNS *by James Hadden*—The French Post Expedition, Great Meadows and Braddock's Defeat—including Braddock's Orderly Books.

BOUQUET & THE OHIO INDIAN WAR *by Cyrus Cort & William Smith*—Two Accounts of the Campaigns of 1763-1764: Bouquet's Campaigns by Cyrus Cort & The History of Bouquet's Expeditions by William Smith.

NARRATIVES OF THE FRENCH & INDIAN WAR: 2 *by David Holden, Samuel Jenks, Lemuel Lyon, Mary Cochrane Rogers & Henry T. Blake*—Contains The Diary of Sergeant David Holden, Captain Samuel Jenks' Journal, The Journal of Lemuel Lyon, Journal of a French Officer at the Siege of Quebec, A Battle Fought on Snowshoes & The Battle of Lake George.

NARRATIVES OF THE FRENCH & INDIAN WAR *by Brown, Eastburn, Hawks & Putnam*—Ranger Brown's Narrative, The Adventures of Robert Eastburn, The Journal of Rufus Putnam—Provincial Infantry & Orderly Book and Journal of Major John Hawks on the Ticonderoga-Crown Point Campaign.

THE 7TH (QUEEN'S OWN) HUSSARS: Volume 1—1688-1792 *by C. R. B. Barrett*—As Dragoons During the Flanders Campaign, War of the Austrian Succession and the Seven Years War.

INDIA'S FREE LANCES *by H. G. Keene*—European Mercenary Commanders in Hindustan 1770-1820.

THE BENGAL EUROPEAN REGIMENT *by P. R. Innes*—An Elite Regiment of the Honourable East India Company 1756-1858.

MUSKET & TOMAHAWK *by Francis Parkman*—A Military History of the French & Indian War, 1753-1760.

THE BLACK WATCH AT TICONDEROGA *by Frederick B. Richards*—Campaigns in the French & Indian War.

QUEEN'S RANGERS *by Frederick B. Richards*—John Simcoe and his Rangers During the Revolutionary War for America.

ALSO FROM LEONAUR
AVAILABLE IN SOFTCOVER OR HARDCOVER WITH DUST JACKET

JOURNALS OF ROBERT ROGERS OF THE RANGERS by *Robert Rogers*—The exploits of Rogers & the Rangers in his own words during 1755-1761 in the French & Indian War.

GALLOPING GUNS by *James Young*—The Experiences of an Officer of the Bengal Horse Artillery During the Second Maratha War 1804-1805.

GORDON by *Demetrius Charles Boulger*—The Career of Gordon of Khartoum.

THE BATTLE OF NEW ORLEANS by *Zachary F. Smith*—The final major engagement of the War of 1812.

THE TWO WARS OF MRS DUBERLY by *Frances Isabella Duberly*—An Intrepid Victorian Lady's Experience of the Crimea and Indian Mutiny.

WITH THE GUARDS' BRIGADE DURING THE BOER WAR by *Edward P. Lowry*—On Campaign from Bloemfontein to Koomati Poort and Back.

THE REBELLIOUS DUCHESS by *Paul F. S. Dermoncourt*—The Adventures of the Duchess of Berri and Her Attempt to Overthrow French Monarchy.

MEN OF THE MUTINY by *John Tulloch Nash & Henry Metcalfe*—Two Accounts of the Great Indian Mutiny of 1857: Fighting with the Bengal Yeomanry Cavalry & Private Metcalfe at Lucknow.

CAMPAIGN IN THE CRIMEA by *George Shuldham Peard*—The Recollections of an Officer of the 20th Regiment of Foot.

WITHIN SEBASTOPOL by *K. Hodasevich*—A Narrative of the Campaign in the Crimea, and of the Events of the Siege.

WITH THE CAVALRY TO AFGHANISTAN by *William Taylor*—The Experiences of a Trooper of H. M. 4th Light Dragoons During the First Afghan War.

THE CAWNPORE MAN by *Mowbray Thompson*—A First Hand Account of the Siege and Massacre During the Indian Mutiny By One of Four Survivors.

BRIGADE COMMANDER: AFGHANISTAN by *Henry Brooke*—The Journal of the Commander of the 2nd Infantry Brigade, Kandahar Field Force During the Second Afghan War.

BANCROFT OF THE BENGAL HORSE ARTILLERY by *N. W. Bancroft*—An Account of the First Sikh War 1845-1846.

AVAILABLE ONLINE AT www.leonaur.com
AND FROM ALL GOOD BOOK STORES

ALSO FROM LEONAUR
AVAILABLE IN SOFTCOVER OR HARDCOVER WITH DUST JACKET

AFGHANISTAN: THE BELEAGUERED BRIGADE *by G. R. Gleig*—An Account of Sale's Brigade During the First Afghan War.

IN THE RANKS OF THE C. I. V *by Erskine Childers*—With the City Imperial Volunteer Battery (Honourable Artillery Company) in the Second Boer War.

THE BENGAL NATIVE ARMY *by F. G. Cardew*—An Invaluable Reference Resource.

THE 7TH (QUEEN'S OWN) HUSSARS: Volume 4—1688-1914 *by C. R. B. Barrett*—Uniforms, Equipment, Weapons, Traditions, the Services of Notable Officers and Men & the Appendices to All Volumes—Volume 4: 1688-1914.

THE SWORD OF THE CROWN *by Eric W. Sheppard*—A History of the British Army to 1914.

THE 7TH (QUEEN'S OWN) HUSSARS: Volume 3—**1818-1914** *by C. R. B. Barrett*—On Campaign During the Canadian Rebellion, the Indian Mutiny, the Sudan, Matabeleland, Mashonaland and the Boer War Volume 3: 1818-1914.

THE KHARTOUM CAMPAIGN *by Bennet Burleigh*—A Special Correspondent's View of the Reconquest of the Sudan by British and Egyptian Forces under Kitchener—1898.

EL PUCHERO *by Richard McSherry*—The Letters of a Surgeon of Volunteers During Scott's Campaign of the American-Mexican War 1847-1848.

RIFLEMAN SAHIB *by E. Maude*—The Recollections of an Officer of the Bombay Rifles During the Southern Mahratta Campaign, Second Sikh War, Persian Campaign and Indian Mutiny.

THE KING'S HUSSAR *by Edwin Mole*—The Recollections of a 14th (King's) Hussar During the Victorian Era.

JOHN COMPANY'S CAVALRYMAN *by William Johnson*—The Experiences of a British Soldier in the Crimea, the Persian Campaign and the Indian Mutiny.

COLENSO & DURNFORD'S ZULU WAR *by Frances E. Colenso & Edward Durnford*—The first and possibly the most important history of the Zulu War.

U. S. DRAGOON *by Samuel E. Chamberlain*—Experiences in the Mexican War 1846-48 and on the South Western Frontier.

AVAILABLE ONLINE AT **www.leonaur.com**
AND FROM ALL GOOD BOOK STORES

ALSO FROM LEONAUR
AVAILABLE IN SOFTCOVER OR HARDCOVER WITH DUST JACKET

THE 2ND MAORI WAR: 1860-1861 *by Robert Carey*—The Second Maori War, or First Taranaki War, one more bloody instalment of the conflicts between European settlers and the indigenous Maori people.

A JOURNAL OF THE SECOND SIKH WAR *by Daniel A. Sandford*—The Experiences of an Ensign of the 2nd Bengal European Regiment During the Campaign in the Punjab, India, 1848-49.

THE LIGHT INFANTRY OFFICER *by John H. Cooke*—The Experiences of an Officer of the 43rd Light Infantry in America During the War of 1812.

BUSHVELDT CARBINEERS *by George Witton*—The War Against the Boers in South Africa and the 'Breaker' Morant Incident.

LAKE'S CAMPAIGNS IN INDIA *by Hugh Pearse*—The Second Anglo Maratha War, 1803-1807.

BRITAIN IN AFGHANISTAN 1: THE FIRST AFGHAN WAR 1839-42 *by Archibald Forbes*—From invasion to destruction-a British military disaster.

BRITAIN IN AFGHANISTAN 2: THE SECOND AFGHAN WAR 1878-80 *by Archibald Forbes*—This is the history of the Second Afghan War-another episode of British military history typified by savagery, massacre, siege and battles.

UP AMONG THE PANDIES *by Vivian Dering Majendie*—Experiences of a British Officer on Campaign During the Indian Mutiny, 1857-1858.

MUTINY: 1857 *by James Humphries*—Authentic Voices from the Indian Mutiny-First Hand Accounts of Battles, Sieges and Personal Hardships.

BLOW THE BUGLE, DRAW THE SWORD *by W. H. G. Kingston*—The Wars, Campaigns, Regiments and Soldiers of the British & Indian Armies During the Victorian Era, 1839-1898.

WAR BEYOND THE DRAGON PAGODA *by Major J. J. Snodgrass*—A Personal Narrative of the First Anglo-Burmese War 1824 - 1826.

THE HERO OF ALIWAL *by James Humphries*—The Campaigns of Sir Harry Smith in India, 1843-1846, During the Gwalior War & the First Sikh War.

ALL FOR A SHILLING A DAY *by Donald F. Featherstone*—The story of H.M. 16th, the Queen's Lancers During the first Sikh War 1845-1846.

AVAILABLE ONLINE AT www.leonaur.com
AND FROM ALL GOOD BOOK STORES

ALSO FROM LEONAUR
AVAILABLE IN SOFTCOVER OR HARDCOVER WITH DUST JACKET

THE FALL OF THE MOGHUL EMPIRE OF HINDUSTAN by H. G. Keene—By the beginning of the nineteenth century, as British and Indian armies under Lake and Wellesley dominated the scene, a little over half a century of conflict brought the Moghul Empire to its knees.

LADY SALE'S AFGHANISTAN by Florentia Sale—An Indomitable Victorian Lady's Account of the Retreat from Kabul During the First Afghan War.

THE CAMPAIGN OF MAGENTA AND SOLFERINO 1859 by Harold Carmichael Wylly—The Decisive Conflict for the Unification of Italy.

FRENCH'S CAVALRY CAMPAIGN by J. G. Maydon—A Special Correspondent's View of British Army Mounted Troops During the Boer War.

CAVALRY AT WATERLOO by Sir Evelyn Wood—British Mounted Troops During the Campaign of 1815.

THE SUBALTERN by George Robert Gleig—The Experiences of an Officer of the 85th Light Infantry During the Peninsular War.

NAPOLEON AT BAY, 1814 by F. Loraine Petre—The Campaigns to the Fall of the First Empire.

NAPOLEON AND THE CAMPAIGN OF 1806 by Colonel Vachée—The Napoleonic Method of Organisation and Command to the Battles of Jena & Auerstädt.

THE COMPLETE ADVENTURES IN THE CONNAUGHT RANGERS by William Grattan—The 88th Regiment during the Napoleonic Wars by a Serving Officer.

BUGLER AND OFFICER OF THE RIFLES by William Green & Harry Smith—With the 95th (Rifles) during the Peninsular & Waterloo Campaigns of the Napoleonic Wars.

NAPOLEONIC WAR STORIES by Sir Arthur Quiller-Couch—Tales of soldiers, spies, battles & sieges from the Peninsular & Waterloo campaigns.

CAPTAIN OF THE 95TH (RIFLES) by Jonathan Leach—An officer of Wellington's sharpshooters during the Peninsular, South of France and Waterloo campaigns of the Napoleonic wars.

RIFLEMAN COSTELLO by Edward Costello—The adventures of a soldier of the 95th (Rifles) in the Peninsular & Waterloo Campaigns of the Napoleonic wars.

AVAILABLE ONLINE AT **www.leonaur.com**
AND FROM ALL GOOD BOOK STORES

ALSO FROM LEONAUR
AVAILABLE IN SOFTCOVER OR HARDCOVER WITH DUST JACKET

AT THEM WITH THE BAYONET by *Donald F. Featherstone*—The first Anglo-Sikh War 1845-1846.

STEPHEN CRANE'S BATTLES by *Stephen Crane*—Nine Decisive Battles Recounted by the Author of 'The Red Badge of Courage'.

THE GURKHA WAR by *H. T. Prinsep*—The Anglo-Nepalese Conflict in North East India 1814-1816.

FIRE & BLOOD by *G. R. Gleig*—The burning of Washington & the battle of New Orleans, 1814, through the eyes of a young British soldier.

SOUND ADVANCE! by *Joseph Anderson*—Experiences of an officer of HM 50th regiment in Australia, Burma & the Gwalior war.

THE CAMPAIGN OF THE INDUS by *Thomas Holdsworth*—Experiences of a British Officer of the 2nd (Queen's Royal) Regiment in the Campaign to Place Shah Shuja on the Throne of Afghanistan 1838 - 1840.

WITH THE MADRAS EUROPEAN REGIMENT IN BURMA by *John Butler*—The Experiences of an Officer of the Honourable East India Company's Army During the First Anglo-Burmese War 1824 - 1826.

IN ZULULAND WITH THE BRITISH ARMY by *Charles L. Norris-Newman*—The Anglo-Zulu war of 1879 through the first-hand experiences of a special correspondent.

BESIEGED IN LUCKNOW by *Martin Richard Gubbins*—The first Anglo-Sikh War 1845-1846.

A TIGER ON HORSEBACK by *L. March Phillips*—The Experiences of a Trooper & Officer of Rimington's Guides - The Tigers - during the Anglo-Boer war 1899 - 1902.

SEPOYS, SIEGE & STORM by *Charles John Griffiths*—The Experiences of a young officer of H.M.'s 61st Regiment at Ferozepore, Delhi ridge and at the fall of Delhi during the Indian mutiny 1857.

CAMPAIGNING IN ZULULAND by *W. E. Montague*—Experiences on campaign during the Zulu war of 1879 with the 94th Regiment.

THE STORY OF THE GUIDES by *G.J. Younghusband*—The Exploits of the Soldiers of the famous Indian Army Regiment from the northwest frontier 1847 - 1900.

AVAILABLE ONLINE AT **www.leonaur.com**
AND FROM ALL GOOD BOOK STORES

ALSO FROM LEONAUR
AVAILABLE IN SOFTCOVER OR HARDCOVER WITH DUST JACKET

ZULU: 1879 *by D.C.F. Moodie & the Leonaur Editors*—The Anglo-Zulu War of 1879 from contemporary sources: First Hand Accounts, Interviews, Dispatches, Official Documents & Newspaper Reports.

THE RED DRAGOON *by W.J. Adams*—With the 7th Dragoon Guards in the Cape of Good Hope against the Boers & the Kaffir tribes during the 'war of the axe' 1843-48'.

THE RECOLLECTIONS OF SKINNER OF SKINNER'S HORSE *by James Skinner*—James Skinner and his 'Yellow Boys' Irregular cavalry in the wars of India between the British, Mahratta, Rajput, Mogul, Sikh & Pindarree Forces.

A CAVALRY OFFICER DURING THE SEPOY REVOLT *by A. R. D. Mackenzie*—Experiences with the 3rd Bengal Light Cavalry, the Guides and Sikh Irregular Cavalry from the outbreak to Delhi and Lucknow.

A NORFOLK SOLDIER IN THE FIRST SIKH WAR *by J W Baldwin*—Experiences of a private of H.M. 9th Regiment of Foot in the battles for the Punjab, India 1845-6.

TOMMY ATKINS' WAR STORIES: 14 FIRST HAND ACCOUNTS—Fourteen first hand accounts from the ranks of the British Army during Queen Victoria's Empire.

THE WATERLOO LETTERS *by H. T. Siborne*—Accounts of the Battle by British Officers for its Foremost Historian.

NEY: GENERAL OF CAVALRY VOLUME 1—1769-1799 *by Antoine Bulos*—The Early Career of a Marshal of the First Empire.

NEY: MARSHAL OF FRANCE VOLUME 2—1799-1805 *by Antoine Bulos*—The Early Career of a Marshal of the First Empire.

AIDE-DE-CAMP TO NAPOLEON *by Philippe-Paul de Ségur*—For anyone interested in the Napoleonic Wars this book, written by one who was intimate with the strategies and machinations of the Emperor, will be essential reading.

TWILIGHT OF EMPIRE *by Sir Thomas Ussher & Sir George Cockburn*—Two accounts of Napoleon's Journeys in Exile to Elba and St. Helena: Narrative of Events by Sir Thomas Ussher & Napoleon's Last Voyage: Extract of a diary by Sir George Cockburn.

PRIVATE WHEELER *by William Wheeler*—The letters of a soldier of the 51st Light Infantry during the Peninsular War & at Waterloo.

AVAILABLE ONLINE AT **www.leonaur.com**
AND FROM ALL GOOD BOOK STORES

ALSO FROM LEONAUR
AVAILABLE IN SOFTCOVER OR HARDCOVER WITH DUST JACKET

OFFICERS & GENTLEMEN *by Peter Hawker & William Graham*—Two Accounts of British Officers During the Peninsula War: Officer of Light Dragoons by Peter Hawker & Campaign in Portugal and Spain by William Graham.

THE WALCHEREN EXPEDITION *by Anonymous*—The Experiences of a British Officer of the 81st Regt. During the Campaign in the Low Countries of 1809.

LADIES OF WATERLOO *by Charlotte A. Eaton, Magdalene de Lancey & Juana Smith*—The Experiences of Three Women During the Campaign of 1815: Waterloo Days by Charlotte A. Eaton, A Week at Waterloo by Magdalene de Lancey & Juana's Story by Juana Smith.

JOURNAL OF AN OFFICER IN THE KING'S GERMAN LEGION *by John Frederick Hering*—Recollections of Campaigning During the Napoleonic Wars.

JOURNAL OF AN ARMY SURGEON IN THE PENINSULAR WAR *by Charles Boutflower*—The Recollections of a British Army Medical Man on Campaign During the Napoleonic Wars.

ON CAMPAIGN WITH MOORE AND WELLINGTON *by Anthony Hamilton*—The Experiences of a Soldier of the 43rd Regiment During the Peninsular War.

THE ROAD TO AUSTERLITZ *by R. G. Burton*—Napoleon's Campaign of 1805.

SOLDIERS OF NAPOLEON *by A. J. Doisy De Villargennes & Arthur Chuquet*—The Experiences of the Men of the French First Empire: Under the Eagles by A. J. Doisy De Villargennes & Voices of 1812 by Arthur Chuquet.

INVASION OF FRANCE, 1814 *by F. W. O. Maycock*—The Final Battles of the Napoleonic First Empire.

LEIPZIG—A CONFLICT OF TITANS *by Frederic Shoberl*—A Personal Experience of the 'Battle of the Nations' During the Napoleonic Wars, October 14th-19th, 1813.

SLASHERS *by Charles Cadell*—The Campaigns of the 28th Regiment of Foot During the Napoleonic Wars by a Serving Officer.

BATTLE IMPERIAL *by Charles William Vane*—The Campaigns in Germany & France for the Defeat of Napoleon 1813-1814.

SWIFT & BOLD *by Gibbes Rigaud*—The 60th Rifles During the Peninsula War.

AVAILABLE ONLINE AT **www.leonaur.com**
AND FROM ALL GOOD BOOK STORES

ALSO FROM LEONAUR
AVAILABLE IN SOFTCOVER OR HARDCOVER WITH DUST JACKET

ADVENTURES OF A YOUNG RIFLEMAN *by Johann Christian Maempel*—The Experiences of a Saxon in the French & British Armies During the Napoleonic Wars.

THE HUSSAR *by Norbert Landsheit & G. R. Gleig*—A German Cavalryman in British Service Throughout the Napoleonic Wars.

RECOLLECTIONS OF THE PENINSULA *by Moyle Sherer*—An Officer of the 34th Regiment of Foot—'The Cumberland Gentlemen'—on Campaign Against Napoleon's French Army in Spain.

MARINE OF REVOLUTION & CONSULATE *by Moreau de Jonnès*—The Recollections of a French Soldier of the Revolutionary Wars 1791-1804.

GENTLEMEN IN RED *by John Dobbs & Robert Knowles*—Two Accounts of British Infantry Officers During the Peninsular War Recollections of an Old 52nd Man by John Dobbs An Officer of Fusiliers by Robert Knowles.

CORPORAL BROWN'S CAMPAIGNS IN THE LOW COUNTRIES *by Robert Brown*—Recollections of a Coldstream Guard in the Early Campaigns Against Revolutionary France 1793-1795.

THE 7TH (QUEENS OWN) HUSSARS: Volume 2—1793-1815 *by C. R. B. Barrett*—During the Campaigns in the Low Countries & the Peninsula and Waterloo Campaigns of the Napoleonic Wars. Volume 2: 1793-1815.

THE MARENGO CAMPAIGN 1800 *by Herbert H. Sargent*—The Victory that Completed the Austrian Defeat in Italy.

DONALDSON OF THE 94TH—SCOTS BRIGADE *by Joseph Donaldson*—The Recollections of a Soldier During the Peninsula & South of France Campaigns of the Napoleonic Wars.

A CONSCRIPT FOR EMPIRE *by Philippe as told to Johann Christian Maempel*—The Experiences of a Young German Conscript During the Napoleonic Wars.

JOURNAL OF THE CAMPAIGN OF 1815 *by Alexander Cavalié Mercer*—The Experiences of an Officer of the Royal Horse Artillery During the Waterloo Campaign.

NAPOLEON'S CAMPAIGNS IN POLAND 1806-7 *by Robert Wilson*—The campaign in Poland from the Russian side of the conflict.

AVAILABLE ONLINE AT **www.leonaur.com**
AND FROM ALL GOOD BOOK STORES

ALSO FROM LEONAUR
AVAILABLE IN SOFTCOVER OR HARDCOVER WITH DUST JACKET

OMPTEDA OF THE KING'S GERMAN LEGION *by Christian von Ompteda*—A Hanoverian Officer on Campaign Against Napoleon.

LIEUTENANT SIMMONS OF THE 95TH (RIFLES) *by George Simmons*—Recollections of the Peninsula, South of France & Waterloo Campaigns of the Napoleonic Wars.

A HORSEMAN FOR THE EMPEROR *by Jean Baptiste Gazzola*—A Cavalryman of Napoleon's Army on Campaign Throughout the Napoleonic Wars.

SERGEANT LAWRENCE *by William Lawrence*—With the 40th Regt. of Foot in South America, the Peninsular War & at Waterloo.

CAMPAIGNS WITH THE FIELD TRAIN *by Richard D. Henegan*—Experiences of a British Officer During the Peninsula and Waterloo Campaigns of the Napoleonic Wars.

CAVALRY SURGEON *by S. D. Broughton*—On Campaign Against Napoleon in the Peninsula & South of France During the Napoleonic Wars 1812-1814.

MEN OF THE RIFLES *by Thomas Knight, Henry Curling & Jonathan Leach*—The Reminiscences of Thomas Knight of the 95th (Rifles) by Thomas Knight, Henry Curling's Anecdotes by Henry Curling & The Field Services of the Rifle Brigade from its Formation to Waterloo by Jonathan Leach.

THE ULM CAMPAIGN 1805 *by F. N. Maude*—Napoleon and the Defeat of the Austrian Army During the 'War of the Third Coalition'.

SOLDIERING WITH THE 'DIVISION' *by Thomas Garrety*—The Military Experiences of an Infantryman of the 43rd Regiment During the Napoleonic Wars.

SERGEANT MORRIS OF THE 73RD FOOT *by Thomas Morris*—The Experiences of a British Infantryman During the Napoleonic Wars-Including Campaigns in Germany and at Waterloo.

A VOICE FROM WATERLOO *by Edward Cotton*—The Personal Experiences of a British Cavalryman Who Became a Battlefield Guide and Authority on the Campaign of 1815.

NAPOLEON AND HIS MARSHALS *by J. T. Headley*—The Men of the First Empire.

AVAILABLE ONLINE AT www.leonaur.com
AND FROM ALL GOOD BOOK STORES

ALSO FROM LEONAUR
AVAILABLE IN SOFTCOVER OR HARDCOVER WITH DUST JACKET

COLBORNE: A SINGULAR TALENT FOR WAR by *John Colborne*—The Napoleonic Wars Career of One of Wellington's Most Highly Valued Officers in Egypt, Holland, Italy, the Peninsula and at Waterloo.

NAPOLEON'S RUSSIAN CAMPAIGN by *Philippe Henri de Segur*—The Invasion, Battles and Retreat by an Aide-de-Camp on the Emperor's Staff.

WITH THE LIGHT DIVISION by *John H. Cooke*—The Experiences of an Officer of the 43rd Light Infantry in the Peninsula and South of France During the Napoleonic Wars.

WELLINGTON AND THE PYRENEES CAMPAIGN VOLUME I: FROM VITORIA TO THE BIDASSOA by *F. C. Beatson*—The final phase of the campaign in the Iberian Peninsula.

WELLINGTON AND THE INVASION OF FRANCE VOLUME II: THE BIDASSOA TO THE BATTLE OF THE NIVELLE by *F. C. Beatson*—The final phase of the campaign in the Iberian Peninsula.

WELLINGTON AND THE FALL OF FRANCE VOLUME III: THE GAVES AND THE BATTLE OF ORTHEZ by *F. C. Beatson*—The final phase of the campaign in the Iberian Peninsula.

NAPOLEON'S IMPERIAL GUARD: FROM MARENGO TO WATERLOO by *J. T. Headley*—The story of Napoleon's Imperial Guard and the men who commanded them.

BATTLES & SIEGES OF THE PENINSULAR WAR by *W. H. Fitchett*—Corunna, Busaco, Albuera, Ciudad Rodrigo, Badajos, Salamanca, San Sebastian & Others.

SERGEANT GUILLEMARD: THE MAN WHO SHOT NELSON? by *Robert Guillemard*—A Soldier of the Infantry of the French Army of Napoleon on Campaign Throughout Europe.

WITH THE GUARDS ACROSS THE PYRENEES by *Robert Batty*—The Experiences of a British Officer of Wellington's Army During the Battles for the Fall of Napoleonic France, 1813.

A STAFF OFFICER IN THE PENINSULA by *E. W. Buckham*—An Officer of the British Staff Corps Cavalry During the Peninsula Campaign of the Napoleonic Wars.

THE LEIPZIG CAMPAIGN: 1813—NAPOLEON AND THE "BATTLE OF THE NATIONS" by *F. N. Maude*—Colonel Maude's analysis of Napoleon's campaign of 1813 around Leipzig.

AVAILABLE ONLINE AT **www.leonaur.com**
AND FROM ALL GOOD BOOK STORES

ALSO FROM LEONAUR
AVAILABLE IN SOFTCOVER OR HARDCOVER WITH DUST JACKET

BUGEAUD: A PACK WITH A BATON *by Thomas Robert Bugeaud*—The Early Campaigns of a Soldier of Napoleon's Army Who Would Become a Marshal of France.

WATERLOO RECOLLECTIONS *by Frederick Llewellyn*—Rare First Hand Accounts, Letters, Reports and Retellings from the Campaign of 1815.

SERGEANT NICOL *by Daniel Nicol*—The Experiences of a Gordon Highlander During the Napoleonic Wars in Egypt, the Peninsula and France.

THE JENA CAMPAIGN: 1806 *by F. N. Maude*—The Twin Battles of Jena & Auerstadt Between Napoleon's French and the Prussian Army.

PRIVATE O'NEIL *by Charles O'Neil*—The recollections of an Irish Rogue of H. M. 28th Regt.—The Slashers—during the Peninsula & Waterloo campaigns of the Napoleonic war.

ROYAL HIGHLANDER *by James Anton*—A soldier of H.M 42nd (Royal) Highlanders during the Peninsular, South of France & Waterloo Campaigns of the Napoleonic Wars.

CAPTAIN BLAZE *by Elzéar Blaze*—Life in Napoleons Army.

LEJEUNE VOLUME 1 *by Louis-François Lejeune*—The Napoleonic Wars through the Experiences of an Officer on Berthier's Staff.

LEJEUNE VOLUME 2 *by Louis-François Lejeune*—The Napoleonic Wars through the Experiences of an Officer on Berthier's Staff.

CAPTAIN COIGNET *by Jean-Roch Coignet*—A Soldier of Napoleon's Imperial Guard from the Italian Campaign to Russia and Waterloo.

FUSILIER COOPER *by John S. Cooper*—Experiences in the 7th (Royal) Fusiliers During the Peninsular Campaign of the Napoleonic Wars and the American Campaign to New Orleans.

FIGHTING NAPOLEON'S EMPIRE *by Joseph Anderson*—The Campaigns of a British Infantryman in Italy, Egypt, the Peninsular & the West Indies During the Napoleonic Wars.

CHASSEUR BARRES *by Jean-Baptiste Barres*—The experiences of a French Infantryman of the Imperial Guard at Austerlitz, Jena, Eylau, Friedland, in the Peninsular, Lutzen, Bautzen, Zinnwald and Hanau during the Napoleonic Wars.

AVAILABLE ONLINE AT **www.leonaur.com**
AND FROM ALL GOOD BOOK STORES

ALSO FROM LEONAUR
AVAILABLE IN SOFTCOVER OR HARDCOVER WITH DUST JACKET

CAPTAIN COIGNET *by Jean-Roch Coignet*—A Soldier of Napoleon's Imperial Guard from the Italian Campaign to Russia and Waterloo.

HUSSAR ROCCA *by Albert Jean Michel de Rocca*—A French cavalry officer's experiences of the Napoleonic Wars and his views on the Peninsular Campaigns against the Spanish, British And Guerilla Armies.

MARINES TO 95TH (RIFLES) *by Thomas Fernyhough*—The military experiences of Robert Fernyhough during the Napoleonic Wars.

LIGHT BOB *by Robert Blakeney*—The experiences of a young officer in H.M 28th & 36th regiments of the British Infantry during the Peninsular Campaign of the Napoleonic Wars 1804 - 1814.

WITH WELLINGTON'S LIGHT CAVALRY *by William Tomkinson*—The Experiences of an officer of the 16th Light Dragoons in the Peninsular and Waterloo campaigns of the Napoleonic Wars.

SERGEANT BOURGOGNE *by Adrien Bourgogne*—With Napoleon's Imperial Guard in the Russian Campaign and on the Retreat from Moscow 1812 - 13.

SURTEES OF THE 95TH (RIFLES) *by William Surtees*—A Soldier of the 95th (Rifles) in the Peninsular campaign of the Napoleonic Wars.

SWORDS OF HONOUR *by Henry Newbolt & Stanley L. Wood*—The Careers of Six Outstanding Officers from the Napoleonic Wars, the Wars for India and the American Civil War.

ENSIGN BELL IN THE PENINSULAR WAR *by George Bell*—The Experiences of a young British Soldier of the 34th Regiment 'The Cumberland Gentlemen' in the Napoleonic wars.

HUSSAR IN WINTER *by Alexander Gordon*—A British Cavalry Officer during the retreat to Corunna in the Peninsular campaign of the Napoleonic Wars.

THE COMPLEAT RIFLEMAN HARRIS *by Benjamin Harris as told to and transcribed by Captain Henry Curling, 52nd Regt. of Foot*—The adventures of a soldier of the 95th (Rifles) during the Peninsular Campaign of the Napoleonic Wars.

THE ADVENTURES OF A LIGHT DRAGOON *by George Farmer & G.R. Gleig*—A cavalryman during the Peninsular & Waterloo Campaigns, in captivity & at the siege of Bhurtpore, India.

AVAILABLE ONLINE AT **www.leonaur.com**
AND FROM ALL GOOD BOOK STORES

ALSO FROM LEONAUR
AVAILABLE IN SOFTCOVER OR HARDCOVER WITH DUST JACKET

THE LIFE OF THE REAL BRIGADIER GERARD VOLUME 1—THE YOUNG HUSSAR 1782-1807 *by Jean-Baptiste De Marbot*—A French Cavalryman Of the Napoleonic Wars at Marengo, Austerlitz, Jena, Eylau & Friedland.

THE LIFE OF THE REAL BRIGADIER GERARD VOLUME 2—IMPERIAL AIDE-DE-CAMP 1807-1811 *by Jean-Baptiste De Marbot*—A French Cavalryman of the Napoleonic Wars at Saragossa, Landshut, Eckmuhl, Ratisbon, Aspern-Essling, Wagram, Busaco & Torres Vedras.

THE LIFE OF THE REAL BRIGADIER GERARD VOLUME 3—COLONEL OF CHASSEURS 1811-1815 *by Jean-Baptiste De Marbot*—A French Cavalryman in the retreat from Moscow, Lutzen, Bautzen, Katzbach, Leipzig, Hanau & Waterloo.

THE INDIAN WAR OF 1864 *by Eugene Ware*—The Experiences of a Young Officer of the 7th Iowa Cavalry on the Western Frontier During the Civil War.

THE MARCH OF DESTINY *by Charles E. Young & V. Devinny*—Dangers of the Trail in 1865 by Charles E. Young & The Story of a Pioneer by V. Devinny, two Accounts of Early Emigrants to Colorado.

CROSSING THE PLAINS *by William Audley Maxwell*—A First Hand Narrative of the Early Pioneer Trail to California in 1857.

CHIEF OF SCOUTS *by William F. Drannan*—A Pilot to Emigrant and Government Trains, Across the Plains of the Western Frontier.

THIRTY-ONE YEARS ON THE PLAINS AND IN THE MOUNTAINS *by William F. Drannan*—William Drannan was born to be a pioneer, hunter, trapper and wagon train guide during the momentous days of the Great American West.

THE INDIAN WARS VOLUNTEER *by William Thompson*—Recollections of the Conflict Against the Snakes, Shoshone, Bannocks, Modocs and Other Native Tribes of the American North West.

THE 4TH TENNESSEE CAVALRY *by George B. Guild*—The Services of Smith's Regiment of Confederate Cavalry by One of its Officers.

COLONEL WORTHINGTON'S SHILOH *by T. Worthington*—The Tennessee Campaign, 1862, by an Officer of the Ohio Volunteers.

FOUR YEARS IN THE SADDLE *by W. L. Curry*—The History of the First Regiment Ohio Volunteer Cavalry in the American Civil War.

AVAILABLE ONLINE AT **www.leonaur.com**
AND FROM ALL GOOD BOOK STORES

ALSO FROM LEONAUR
AVAILABLE IN SOFTCOVER OR HARDCOVER WITH DUST JACKET

LIFE IN THE ARMY OF NORTHERN VIRGINIA *by Carlton McCarthy*—The Observations of a Confederate Artilleryman of Cutshaw's Battalion During the American Civil War 1861-1865.

HISTORY OF THE CAVALRY OF THE ARMY OF THE POTOMAC *by Charles D. Rhodes*—Including Pope's Army of Virginia and the Cavalry Operations in West Virginia During the American Civil War.

CAMP-FIRE AND COTTON-FIELD *by Thomas W. Knox*—A New York Herald Correspondent's View of the American Civil War.

SERGEANT STILLWELL *by Leander Stillwell* —The Experiences of a Union Army Soldier of the 61st Illinois Infantry During the American Civil War.

STONEWALL'S CANNONEER *by Edward A. Moore*—Experiences with the Rockbridge Artillery, Confederate Army of Northern Virginia, During the American Civil War.

THE SIXTH CORPS *by George Stevens*—The Army of the Potomac, Union Army, During the American Civil War.

THE RAILROAD RAIDERS *by William Pittenger*—An Ohio Volunteers Recollections of the Andrews Raid to Disrupt the Confederate Railroad in Georgia During the American Civil War.

CITIZEN SOLDIER *by John Beatty*—An Account of the American Civil War by a Union Infantry Officer of Ohio Volunteers Who Became a Brigadier General.

COX: PERSONAL RECOLLECTIONS OF THE CIVIL WAR--VOLUME 1 *by Jacob Dolson Cox*—West Virginia, Kanawha Valley, Gauley Bridge, Cotton Mountain, South Mountain, Antietam, the Morgan Raid & the East Tennessee Campaign.

COX: PERSONAL RECOLLECTIONS OF THE CIVIL WAR--VOLUME 2 *by Jacob Dolson Cox*—Siege of Knoxville, East Tennessee, Atlanta Campaign, the Nashville Campaign & the North Carolina Campaign.

KERSHAW'S BRIGADE VOLUME 1 *by D. Augustus Dickert*—Manassas, Seven Pines, Sharpsburg (Antietam), Fredricksburg, Chancellorsville, Gettysburg, Chickamauga, Chattanooga, Fort Sanders & Bean Station.

KERSHAW'S BRIGADE VOLUME 2 *by D. Augustus Dickert*—At the wilderness, Cold Harbour, Petersburg, The Shenandoah Valley and Cedar Creek..

AVAILABLE ONLINE AT **www.leonaur.com**
AND FROM ALL GOOD BOOK STORES

ALSO FROM LEONAUR
AVAILABLE IN SOFTCOVER OR HARDCOVER WITH DUST JACKET

ESCAPE FROM THE FRENCH *by Edward Boys*—A Young Royal Navy Midshipman's Adventures During the Napoleonic War.

THE VOYAGE OF H.M.S. PANDORA *by Edward Edwards R. N. & George Hamilton, edited by Basil Thomson*—In Pursuit of the Mutineers of the Bounty in the South Seas—1790-1791.

MEDUSA *by J. B. Henry Savigny and Alexander Correard and Charlotte-Adélaïde Dard*—Narrative of a Voyage to Senegal in 1816 & The Sufferings of the Picard Family After the Shipwreck of the Medusa.

THE SEA WAR OF 1812 VOLUME 1 *by A. T. Mahan*—A History of the Maritime Conflict.

THE SEA WAR OF 1812 VOLUME 2 *by A. T. Mahan*—A History of the Maritime Conflict.

WETHERELL OF H. M. S. HUSSAR *by John Wetherell*—The Recollections of an Ordinary Seaman of the Royal Navy During the Napoleonic Wars.

THE NAVAL BRIGADE IN NATAL *by C. R. N. Burne*—With the Guns of H. M. S. Terrible & H. M. S. Tartar during the Boer War 1899-1900.

THE VOYAGE OF H. M. S. BOUNTY *by William Bligh*—The True Story of an 18th Century Voyage of Exploration and Mutiny.

SHIPWRECK! *by William Gilly*—The Royal Navy's Disasters at Sea 1793-1849.

KING'S CUTTERS AND SMUGGLERS: 1700-1855 *by E. Keble Chatterton*—A unique period of maritime history-from the beginning of the eighteenth to the middle of the nineteenth century when British seamen risked all to smuggle valuable goods from wool to tea and spirits from and to the Continent.

CONFEDERATE BLOCKADE RUNNER *by John Wilkinson*—The Personal Recollections of an Officer of the Confederate Navy.

NAVAL BATTLES OF THE NAPOLEONIC WARS *by W. H. Fitchett*—Cape St. Vincent, the Nile, Cadiz, Copenhagen, Trafalgar & Others.

PRISONERS OF THE RED DESERT *by R. S. Gwatkin-Williams*—The Adventures of the Crew of the Tara During the First World War.

U-BOAT WAR 1914-1918 *by James B. Connolly/Karl von Schenk*—Two Contrasting Accounts from Both Sides of the Conflict at Sea During the Great War.

AVAILABLE ONLINE AT www.leonaur.com
AND FROM ALL GOOD BOOK STORES

www.ingramcontent.com/pod-product-compliance
Lightning Source LLC
Chambersburg PA
CBHW021003090426
42738CB00007B/635